PIME in North America

FIFTY YEARS

Presence and Impact

PIME IN NORTH AMERICA

FIFTY YEARS

Presence and Impact

Piero Gheddo

PIME
WORLD
PRESS
Detroit, Michigan

PIME World Press
17330 Quincy St.
Detroit, Michigan 48221-2765

Printed in U.S.A.
Library of Congress Catalog Card Number: 97-076007
ISBN: 0-9642010-6-2

CONTENTS

(CORRECTED PAGINATION)

CONTENTS

ABBREVIATIONS

"Fr." ("Frs." in the plural) is the abbreviation used throughout the book for the priestly title, "Father" ("Fathers"). "Br." ("Brs.") is used for "Brother" ("Brothers"), the title of an unordained member of a religious order or society.

P.I.M.E. and PIME stand for "Pontifical Institute for Foreign Missions" in Latin.

FOREWORD

"I have seen your missionaries at work, and I admire your excellent spirit. I would be happy to see American young men being trained in the spirit of PIME."

(Words of Cardinal Edward Mooney to Fr. Nicholas Maestrini)

Cardinal Mooney and the missions

His Eminence Edward Cardinal Mooney, Archbishop of Detroit from 1937 to 1958, certainly was one of the most influential, farsighted, and dynamic personalities of the U.S. Catholic church throughout the 1940s and 1950s. His training in Rome as a student, his many years in the diplomatic corps of the Vatican, his time in India (1926–1931) and Japan (1931–1933) as apostolic delegate[1] gave him a vision of worldwide Christianity and an interest in the foreign missions, probably unparalleled by any other dignitary of the church at that time.

Among the innumerable decisions that he made every day as archbishop of Detroit, there was one that influenced millions of lives and had global repercussions: his decision in 1947 to invite PIME to set up a

---

[1] The representative of the pope in countries that do not have diplomatic ties with the Vatican.

branch in the United States. He invited his old friend from his days in Bengal, India, Father Guido Margutti of PIME, to establish the society's residence in his archdiocese, the Archdiocese of Detroit.

This year PIME celebrates the fiftieth anniversary of that happy event, and we, all the members of PIME, want to take this opportunity to thank the hierarchy, the clergy, and above all, the large numbers of people all over America who, throughout the last fifty years, collaborated with us in the development of PIME.

Cardinal Mooney's invitation to Father Margutti was not a casual act of charity made on the spur of the moment to a begging missionary; rather it was the fruit of his vision and interest in the presentation of Christ's message to the non-Christian world and his desire to use the immense resources of this country in men and wealth to promote the advancement of the Kingdom of God in mission lands.

When, in 1953, through the Newman Press, we published our first vocational book, *Forward with Christ*,[2] Cardinal Mooney kindly agreed to write the foreword that follows:

> To be a Catholic means, in reality, to be an apostle — that is, to be concerned with and work for the spread of the Faith. This belongs to the very essence of our religion. Yet how many of us have failed to imbibe this spirit and to make it a living factor in

[2] *Forward with Christ* was the new title of the old book by Fr. Paul Manna, *The Workers are Few, (Operari autem pauci)*, first translated and published in English by the later Msgr. Joseph McGlichey of Boston in 1911. PIME published it under its new title because of the great difference in the missionary situation between 1911 and 1953 that required extensive revision and updating.

our Catholic life! There are even many people who have such a narrow concept of the Christian religion as to think of it merely as a kind of personal safe-conduct or passport to insure their entrance into heaven.

As a result of such thinking, the work of the foreign missions — the work of extending the frontiers of Christ's earthly kingdom — has languished in past centuries and, even today, is all too widely thought of as the special task of a small group of generous souls rather than the joint effort of the whole of Christianity to fulfill the divine command, "Go forth and teach all nations." The truth, of course, is that the work of converting the world and sending more heralds of the gospel to bring the good tidings of salvation to all nations is something which should be of deep interest to every thinking Catholic.

This was Cardinal Mooney's vision of the role of foreign missions in Catholic life, and he did not limit himself to mere lip service; he translated his belief into action.

Cardinal Mooney and PIME

There were two factors that influenced Cardinal Mooney's invitation to PIME to establish a branch in the United States: first, as I mentioned above, his genuine and enlightened interest in the missions; and secondly, his personal and high regard for both Father Margutti and the many PIME missionaries he had met in India, Burma, and Hong Kong. In the foreword quoted above, he describes mission life as he saw and experienced it in his visits to the PIME missions in the Far East, especially in Bengal, India, and eastern Burma:

> Living with missionaries, sharing their humble living quarters and frugal meals, traveling with them by primitive means of transportation, observing them both in well-established mission centers and on the very frontiers of the Faith, as in upper and eastern Burma, I have had occasion to know at first hand and to admire their inspiring work. I have seen that missionary life requires, indeed, a spirit of dedication and sacrifice, but also a youthful exuberance and enthusiasm. These latter qualities we like to think of as typically American. In war they have made American marines rate high in opening up the way for fleets and armies. In peace they can make American missionaries rate high as soldiers of Christ on the front of lines of God's kingdom.

What Cardinal Mooney describes here is not only the adventurous and primitive life typical of most PIME missionaries with whom he lived on his visits to our missions, but also the spirit of love and sacrifice inherited from the first group of heroic priests, such as Blessed John Mazzucconi, who were the real founders of PIME. It was this genuine spirit of total dedication that impressed Mooney and lead him to say to me on my very first meeting with him in 1951: "I have seen your missionaries at work, and I admire your excellent spirit. I would be happy to see American young men being trained in the spirit of PIME."

Faith in American youth

On that memorable day of August 1947, when Cardinal Mooney invited Father Margutti to open a branch of PIME in the States, probably neither of them had a clear idea of the far-reaching consequences of that offer and how it would soon lead to the internationalization of PIME around the world. But, today, looking in retrospect to that eventful day, we cannot fail to see the hand of God writing history in the world of the foreign missions. That day Mooney and Margutti were thinking primarily of the immediate financial help for the PIME missions devastated by World War II rather than the internationalization of PIME. But that was the mustard seed planted by God, Himself, destined to grow into a very large tree.

Four years later, in August 1951, during my first meeting with the cardinal, the idea of recruiting vocations in the States was first discussed. At that time the financial needs of PIME were no longer as pressing as in 1947, and we soon became oriented more towards vocations than fund-raising as the primary purpose of our presence in the States. Throughout the following years, the good cardinal continued to encourage us to recruit vocations and heartily welcomed our decision to locate our Maryglade college and theological school in his archdiocese because he believed in the lofty ideals of American youth. Let me quote again from the foreword:

> It can never be said that mission life does not appeal or is not suited to our American youth. Well-known facts prove the contrary. The spirit of Catholic America is a youthful spirit, a buoyant, pioneering spirit. The practical skills and organizing ability which have brought our country to

5

the forefront among the nations can also play a decisive role in the life of the church throughout the world. The fact that here in the United States there are now 53 religious societies for men and 67 for women[3] which are recruiting missionary vocations is definite proof that these organizations have faith in the zealous ability of our youth and that they believe in the tremendous potentialities of our country.

There is not one single need of mankind, not one appeal for help which has not, in our day, struck a responsive chord in the hearts of our people and called forth their bountiful help. This is why American youth, once made aware of the tremendous needs, not only for material means but also for consecrated service in the foreign and home mission fields, will not, in my opinion, fail to respond generously. The thousands of former G.I.'s who were inspired by what they saw of mission work in the service of their country abroad and entered missionary orders after their discharge, are evident proof that Christ's call for foreign service makes an alluring appeal to the best of our youth.

With the exception of a few of us who did not favor the recruiting of vocations, about ninety percent of our community fully shared Cardinal Mooney's faith in

---

[3] These were the statistics in 1953. I have no current statistics, but I presume there is not much difference.

American youth — and still do. Throughout these first fifty years, every activity we initiated — and they are many and varied and well described in this book by Father Gheddo — had no other purpose than to foster vocations for the missionary priesthood. Obviously, we had to develop many fund-raising activities to help our missions abroad as well as pay for the building of our seminaries and the education of students, but we have never deviated from our main goal, that of vocations.

Success or failure?

One or two centuries from now, historians will be able to tell whether the first fifty years of PIME in the United States were a success or a failure. What we can say now is that we all — both American and Italian priests and brothers — have tried hard and spared no sacrifice to achieve success. In certain fields, such as fund-raising, promotion, help to the needy people in our missions, and many others, we achieved a measure of success. In others, such as recruiting and keeping vocations, we certainly did not have the success we had hoped. The main reason is that times have changed a great deal since the 1950s and so has American youth. This fact is well documented by vocational statistics nationally. In the early 1950s there were over 50,000 American seminarians in both diocesan and religious seminaries in the United States. Today there are only about 4,000.[4]

Throughout these changing times, dating back to 1965, we all worked, we all prayed, we all suffered. The young Americans who entered our seminaries and left, those faithful who remained, the 150 Italian

---

[4] Statistics by CARA, the Catholic agency for vocational statistics in Washington, D.C.

priests who came, worked in this region, and then went on either to eternal rest or to other missions, have all shared the pain of failure, discomfort, and lack of success. I think especially of the dozens of priests, American and Italians, involved in the educational work in our seminaries and the silent agony they endured, year after year, in carrying out their duties as educators with no apparent result, as practically all the students were leaving even before entering college.

But have we really failed in the eyes of God? Have all the efforts, prayers, and sacrifices endured by us and by so many of our friends been in vain? I emphatically affirm: NO, NOT AT ALL! The death of Jesus on Calvary was certainly a failure in the eyes of people, but in the eyes of God it was the triumph of life over death and the salvation of all humanity. I am confident that our apparent failure, especially in recruiting vocations, is no failure in the eyes of God. Our labors and sufferings cannot be in vain. One day, the good Lord in His own time, in His own way, will grant us success in this crucial field of our work here. The history of almost all the religious societies that have come to the United States from Europe to recruit vocations is pretty much the same: decades and decades of failure, anguish, and disappointment...followed by success.

In the meantime this book by the internationally known mission journalist, Father Piero Gheddo of PIME, is an excellent illustration and presentation of the collaborative work of American and Italian priests,[5] brothers, and students promoting in this

---

[5] As well as all the good sisters from Italy, Malta, and Mexico who worked so faithfully in our seminary kitchens.

country an awareness of the missions through our magazine *PIME World* (formerly *Catholic Life*), educating thousands of youth through school talks (especially at our vocational summer camps) and contributing to the growth of the church in the States. The tremendous amount of support that we sent (to help poor children, the sick, the elderly in need, the orphanages and hospitals; the chapels built; the education of the local clergy), is undoubtedly a success due to the overwhelming generosity of our American friends. This success has exceeded by far even the rosiest of hopes of Cardinal Mooney and Father Margutti fifty years ago. It can be stated that today in the eighteen nations in which PIME is at work — extending from central Brazil to Papua New Guinea, from Africa to East Asia — there are literally millions of people whose lives have been saved, or improved, or spiritually uplifted by the help that our PIME missionaries were able to give because of the generosity of our American friends.

I want to emphasize that this book is dedicated to all our American friends — young and old, rich and poor, Catholics, Jews, Protestants, and Muslims — for their generous and unfailing support. If we are able to present this report of our first fifty years of work in the United States, it is only because our friends in Michigan, Ohio, New Jersey, New Mexico, Florida, California, all over the fifty states, have made it possible for us to do so. Without their incredibly generous help in all fields of our labors we would have not been able to do all we have done for the American church and for the millions of poor people in our missions.

On behalf of each and every member of PIME — past, present, and future — I want to say to all our supporters and benefactors, rich and poor, living and deceased:

God bless you, and reward you a hundred-fold for your charity, your support, your endless hours of work, your dedication, your loyalty, and above all for your prayers and sacrifices that have made PIME an instrument of growth in the Kingdom of God.

Reverend Nicholas Maestrini, PIME

August 26, 1997

INTRODUCTION

THIS YEAR, 1997, THE PONTIFICAL INSTITUTE FOR FOREIGN Missions (PIME), born in 1850 in Saronno Italy, celebrates the fiftieth anniversary of its presence in North America. This book is a commemoration of that event, and is the fruit of a thorough research which I completed in the U.S., Canada and Mexico in April and May of 1997. I interviewed all of the PIME members, as well as many co-workers and friends of the institute; and I read much of the material which has been printed about the presence of PIME in America. Of particular note is Fr. Nicholas Maestrini's book, *PIME in the United States - The First Twenty-five Years, 1947–72.*[1]

I thank Fr. Franco Cagnasso, Superior General of PIME, who invited me to go to America to write this book; Fr. Steve Baumbusch and seminarian Guy Christopher Snyder for the English translation; and Fr. Bruno Piccolo, PIME's U.S. Regional Superior, who accompanied me on my travels, guiding my journalistic research on PIME in North America. I thank also all the confreres and friends whom I met and interviewed.

Fr. Piero Gheddo, PIME
Milan; July 15, 1997

---

[1] PIME World Press; Detroit, 1994; 370 pages.

CHAPTER I

HEROIC TIMES: PIME'S FOUNDATION IN AMERICA (1947–1951)

IN 1947, THE PIME MISSIONARIES CAME TO THE UNITED STATES with the precise purpose of representing PIME and finding economic help for the institute and its missions. Immediately following World War II, PIME was experiencing a period of poverty and devastation which would today be unimaginable. In Italy their houses had been bombed, including the mother house in Milan, while the Asian missions (China, Burma, Hong Kong) had been destroyed by both the war and the expulsion of their missionaries, who were now confined in concentration camps. Many missionaries were returning to Italy from prisons in China, Russia, Burma, India, South Africa, and Kenya; they had nothing, and many were ill and in need of treatment.

A personal memory. I entered PIME in September of 1945 (I was 16 years old) and I studied in the institute's seminaries in Monza, Genoa, and Milan up to my priesthood ordination in 1953. In those years, the poverty of PIME was truly miserable. We students experienced real hunger, some suffered from lung problems (I personally had a bout with pneumonia) due to scarce nourishment and the humid winter cold. There was no heating in our seminaries until the 1950s. During the first years of studies in Monza and Genoa, we had to go into the fields to look underground for carrots and roots to eat raw; at meals they served us the smelly and almost inedible unsold remains of fish from the market. I remember well several nights when we organized "raids" on the seminary kitchen, to eat cold leftover soup (they used to give us only one ladle of it for dinner, and the rest had to be saved for the next day).

Years later, in 1957, while I was studying in Rome, PIME's superior general, Fr. Augusto Lombardi, confided to me: "I should go to visit our missionaries in Japan, Hong Kong, Burma, Pakistan and India, but I don't have the money for an airplane ticket and it would take months by ship. I will go to Propaganda Fide and ask for some Masses to celebrate or a loan..."[1]

Seeking help for PIME and the missions

So this was the situation of the institute when in 1946 the superior general, Bishop Lorenzo Maria Balconi, sent Fr. Guido Margutti to the United States in order to "seek if possible, a foothold for PIME. If we succeed in getting at least Mass stipends it would be a great help. Other religious societies have already done so."[2] Fr. Margutti, a missionary in India, who had been detained in Argentina during the war, was the man best suited for this assignment. "With sparkling eyes," writes Fr. Maestrini, "a broad smile and uncanny ability to make friends (especially with the secretaries of people in high places) he often succeeded where others failed."[3]

In addition, Fr. Guido had a great spirit of faith and

---

[1] In the historical volume, *Mission Brazil — Fifty Years of PIME in the land of the Holy Cross (1947–1957)*, I amply describe the poverty of the first PIME missionaries sent to Brazil and to the Amazon. They sufferend from malnutrition and other resulting illnesses.
[2] Maestrini, op.cit., page 29.
[3] Maestrini, op.cit., page 30.

love for the missions, great humility, and a capacity for sacrifice.

Upon his arrival in New York on September 26, 1946, Fr. Margutti asked to be assigned as an assistant priest in any of the city's parishes where he would have room and board and could send the monthly stipend of one hundred dollars and the Mass offerings (five dollars each) back to Italy; this was a notable sum in hunger-stricken Italy. He obtained permission to live in the rectory of St. Dominic's in the Bronx as an assistant (but without the stipend and Mass offerings). Then he went to St. Patrick's parish in Richmond, there too only on a temporary basis. Margutti visited the apostolic delegation in Washington and various dioceses but was unable to obtain a stable arrangement which allowed him to help the institute and its missions.

He was finally received and welcomed by Cardinal Edward Mooney, Archbishop of Detroit, who cordially opened the doors of the American church. But his misadventures up to that point, from September 26, 1946 to August 20, 1947, are worthy of a soap opera. Hopes and delusions, promises and refusals in many dioceses, enthusiasm and humiliation are all elements of this personal "Way of the Cross" from which was born an American PIME. Fr. Guido felt like, and at times was treated like, a beggar. But he resisted the strong temptation of returning to Italy, especially thinking about the absolute misery of his Bengali people and also, in those times, of PIME in Italy.

When he visited the diocese of Grand Rapids (Michigan), Margutti was able to arrange an appointment with Bishop Francis J. Haas, who was quite busy that day. After hearing that he was a foreign missionary coming from Bengal in order to find American help, Bishop Haas brutally told him, "I am tired of wasting my time with missionaries and mendicant priests from all over the world. Return to your mission and leave me in peace."

The humble yet firm reaction of Margutti reveals his character. Kneeling down to kiss the bishop's ring, he responded, "You are right; if I were in your place I would do the same. It's true, there are too many of us begging missionaries." He said goodbye and began to leave, but he hadn't even reached the door when the bishop called him back and said, "You are very humble and I admire that. You accepted my anger with great humility. Please be seated and let's talk a bit." The two then became friends. The meeting with Bishop Haas was not the only one like this. At times Fr. Guido was received coldly, and other times he was treated harshly. But he was able, with patience and a smile, to disarm the "adversary" and to win a friend.

Cardinal Mooney opens the doors of America to PIME

While Apostolic Delegate in India, Cardinal Edward Mooney had known Margutti and the PIME community. In 1927, he went to Bengal (then known as "the tomb of the white men") where he had wanted to visit the most forsaken districts of the missions in the immense plains surrounded by the great rivers of India: the Ganges, the Brahmaputra, and the Tista.

Afterwards, the young American bishop, diplomat of the Holy See, expressed in a letter his great admiration for the PIME Missionaries and for Fr. Guido. But Fr. Guido tried to minimize the bishop's praise saying, "It doesn't surprise me that he has the idea that I'm a great missionary... The only real missionary experience that the cardinal had ever had during his entire stay in India was to my missionary district in Bengal. We traveled together on a ox-drawn cart and on an elephant, and I accompanied him into the poorest Christian villages, since he had asked to have a truly profound experience of missionary life..."

Mooney, who died in 1958, was one of the most influential persons in the American church of that era, as archbishop of Detroit (1937) and cardinal (February 21, 1946). He invited Fr. Margutti into his diocese and in October 1947 assigned him to the Italian national parish of San Francesco, as an assistant to Fr. Emilio Capano, the Italian pastor. (On January 11, 1949, the parish was entrusted to PIME.) Having found a stable residence, the young Italian missionary began his great activity of mission appeals in the parishes of over 20 dioceses, and asked Fr. Luigi Risso, the superior general, for some other missionaries to help him; numerous dioceses had granted him permission for these mission appeals and he couldn't cover them all by himself.

At the beginning of 1949, his first assistant arrived: Fr. Carlo Sala, who had been a missionary in Ethiopia. In that same year five others would follow: Frs. Andrea Granelli (from Hong Kong), Luigi Vigano (from Brazil), Dante Magri and Mario Dell'Agnol (from India), and the young priest Fr. Casto Marrapese (from Italy).

Margutti makes peace between the Italians and the bishop of Columbus

In the meantime, PIME was working not only in the parish of San Francesco in Detroit but also in Columbus, Ohio. The bishop of Columbus, like many other bishops of those years, was against the national parishes, which didn't have well-defined territories but rather were for the immigrants of foreign nations who had not been fully integrated into American society. There were parishes for Italians, Germans, Poles, French, etc. In

16

the 1940s and 1950s, the American church was abolishing these parishes. Today, however, due to the new waves of immigration (Latin-American, Chinese, Vietnamese, Indian, Filipino, etc.), it seems we're returning to these parishes with different languages and cultures (now no longer called national parishes but personal parishes).

In Columbus there was (and is today) a strong Italian community in the parish of St. John the Baptist. At that time an extraordinary man, who was loved by his faithful, was pastor (and had been since 1913). His name was Fr. Rocco Petrarca, a diocesan priest from Bordighera, Imperia (Italy), who was a doctor, music composer, writer, architect — and a good priest. Fr. Petrarca became ill in 1947 and had to leave the parish. It remained one year without a priest because the bishop, Michael J. Ready, wanted to close the Italian parish. He therefore assigned a priest from the seminary to the church, giving him the task of taking care of all pending affairs and closing the church.

But the good American bishop didn't know about the proud and rebellious Italian spirit! They threatened to occupy the church (remember, this was 1948, not 1968!) and to run it independently of the bishop; for this reason they sent a commission to the Vatican, where they understood they would find firm support.

Alarmed by the way things were proceeding, Ready went to Cardinal Mooney, his mentor and good friend, asking for his advice. Mooney sent him Fr. Guido Margutti, who remained in Columbus for only a few weeks; he visited the Italian families and institutions, set up meetings with those leading the protest, and was able to make peace.

Many years later, Fr. Maestrini recalls, "the parishioners remembered Fr. Margutti and the way he used to

17

travel the streets of the city — badly dressed and trembling — in order to visit the sick. His contagious smile, his humor, and his natural good sense conquered the hearts of the faithful."

On August 5, 1948, on the advice of Cardinal Mooney, Bishop Ready phoned Margutti. He told him that he was ready to entrust the Italian parish of Saint John the Baptist to PIME. In fact, since there were two Italian parishes in the city, he proposed that PIME take over both of them.

Adaptation to American culture is a must

At the beginning of 1949, then, PIME could say that it was pretty well established in the United States, just one and half years after the arrival of its first missionary. Surely there were difficulties with the American culture, but the esteem and the support of Cardinal Mooney helped to resolve these problems.[4]

The superior general, Fr. Luigi Risso, visited the

---

[4] In the autumn of 1948, Bishop Thomas Malloy of Brooklyn, New York, protested to Cardinal Mooney because Fr. Margutti was sending letters from Detroit with the name "Pontifical Society for the Foreign Missions of Milan," and this name was being confused with that of the "Pontifical Society for the Propagation of the Faith." Mooney responded clarifying the issue and expressing the great esteem he held for PIME and its missionaries whom he had seen working in India and Burma. But the national director of the Propagation of the Faith, Bishop Thomas J. McDonnel, wrote protesting to Propaganda Fide, which had approved the founding of PIME in the United States.

An exchange of letters began between Cardinal Mooney and Monsignor Leo DeBarry (secretary of the Propagation of the Faith for the Detroit Diocese) on one side and the representatives of the Propagation of the Faith in America on the other. The former defended the right of PIME to call itself by the institute's official title which had been approved by the Holy See. The latter claimed that PIME had to avoid every confusion in its use of a name. Margutti adopted the title: "The American Branch of the Milan Pontifical Society for the Foreign Missions." In August 1951 PIME in America assumed the name of "Sts. Peter and Paul Missionaries", but at the end of the 1950s the superior general, Fr. Augusto Lombardi, approved the official title "PIME" for the United States, too.

United States and, returning to Rome, decided with his council to recall Fr. Margutti to Italy. He advised Cardinal Mooney on August 22, 1949 that Fr. Margutti was being reassigned. Margutti was advised to help Fr. Dante Magri, the pastor of the cathedral in Hyderabad, India, who was being sent to the United States to take his place.

What happened? Different episodes and misunderstandings can today make this decision seem incomprehensible. But at the base of it all, putting aside peoples' different characters, there were internal contrasts of a cultural and "ideological" nature among the missionaries sent to the United States. Beginning in the summer of 1947, Fr. Margutti had asked Fr. Risso to send him some more missionaries to help; he wanted those missionaries who were able to adapt well to the American mentality, and he added, "Keep in mind that the religious superiors of European societies must necessarily adopt the American mentality when they have to make decisions about America. Otherwise serious blunders will be made."

Maestrini comments, "Fr. Margutti was absolutely right. But how could the superiors of PIME in Italy, who had never visited the States, and who had been educated in a strict Latin culture, all at once assume an American mentality? Throughout the rest of his stay in the States, Fr. Margutti and later his successors, Fathers Magri and I, had to face the almost impossible task of getting the PIME superiors in Italy to see things from the American perspective and to decide matters accordingly. Of course, this situation is not peculiar to PIME but is common to all religious societies from Europe which open branches here. It is certainly a proof of God's guidance that many of these societies have grown and developed, as PIME did, in spite of blunders caused by the deep-rooted differences between the Latin and Anglo-Saxon mentalities."[5]

So what provoked Fr. Margutti's recall to Italy? There is substantially only one thing: Margutti had come to America with the purpose of finding help for PIME and its missions, doing some missionary promotion work in the American church, and making friends for the institute and the missions. In order to do this, he had wanted collaborators who were profoundly incarnated into the American reality and mentality.

The other missionaries (except the young priests, like Marrapese, for whom this was their first assignment) came to America in order to do that which they had done in their missions: being resident pastors with a flock to care for. Margutti tried to accommodate himself to many American dioceses and ecclesial institutions and, from the beginning, was almost forced to acculturate into the American mentality, culture, and language since he had no stable residence or apostolate. The others who came later found themselves in one of PIME's houses or in a parish and continued to do that which they had always done well (since the missionaries sent to the United States were usually excellent priests): being pastors of souls without worrying too much (or not being young enough) about learning well American English (which is different from the English spoken in India, Burma, Hong Kong, etc.), American customs, the American mentality, etc.

Therefore, Margutti was thinking about the big picture, making big plans, visiting new dioceses, encouraging his confreres to take up new initiatives, to write articles and speak on the radio, to hold conferences and

---

5 Maestrini, op. cit., page 41.

mission appeals — even in distant cities where there were no PIME residences. He wanted the missionaries to be not just pastors but promoters[6]. This ended up bothering those who, because of their not being so young and not having specific experience in missionary promotion, conceived of our presence in America as only pastoral activity within a parish and with a precise and well-defined flock.[7]

Father Guido founded PIME in America

Monsignor Leo DeBarry, director of the Propagation of the Faith in the Diocese of Detroit, wrote a long and blunt letter of protest to Fr. Luigi Risso on September 30, 1949 (having evidently consulted his archbishop first). Recalling Fr. Guido Margutti to Italy was a mistaken decision; he was very well known and esteemed, and nobody could take his place of representing PIME in America. DeBarry excused himself for being so frank,

---

[6] In a letter to Fr. Risso dated August 21, 1948, right after he had been received by Cardinal Mooney (who had opened the doors of the American church for him), Margutti asked for "a priest who is able to speak on the radio, who is able to write articles for newspapers and for missionary magazines and can establish a friendly relationship with all the directors of the Propagation of the Faith." That is, he wanted a priest who was a missionary animator, not simply a pastor of souls! (See the quoted volume of Maestrini, pages 40–41.)

[7] One example of this is the arrival of 19 young PIME missionaries in the United States on August 30, 1947. They were going from Italy to China by way of the Panama Canal on an American ship. They stopped twelve days in New York and Margutti saw it as a good occasion for making PIME known. Early on he made the arrangements for an audience with Cardinal Spellman, a press interview, and radio and TV. coverage. But the 19 young priests, as soon as they disembarked, rather than following Margutti who wanted to take them to stay with the Maryknoll Missionaries in Ossining, began to visit New York on their own, wearing the long cassocks which were common in Italy at that time. The day after, the newspapers printed pictures and stories of this curious invasion of "aliens" on the streets of the metropolis, with their long beards and strange clothing. It was negative publicity for PIME. After this, it was no longer worthwhile to insist upon press conferences and radio or television coverage.

but believed that the missionaries sent to help Margutti were either ill or not well adapted to the task, and were very limited in the amount of time they had to act. Risso tried to reverse his decision, telling Margutti to stay on in America a little while longer as procurator. However, Fr. Margutti, ill and already prepared to leave, returned to Italy; there he directed and strengthened PIME's missionary museum in Milan until his death on July 17, 1972.

"Many years after his return to Italy," writes Fr. Maestrini, "Fr. Margutti would tell story after story of the heroic days when he had founded PIME in the States. Listening to him, one could hardly fail to be impressed with his indomitable spirit, his energy and, above all, his spirit of sacrifice. He was the real founder of PIME in the States and he founded it on the true Christian bases of spiritual sacrifice and total dedication to the missionary ideal."[8]

Maestrini gives a summary of Margutti's stay in America (three years: September 26, 1946 to October 1949). Starting from scratch, he left PIME in the U.S. with two parishes entrusted to it in Detroit and Columbus, a residence for the institute, and good relations with various dioceses and diocesan missionary offices. The latter assigned to the institute as many mission appeals as it was able to preach each year.

The purpose for which the superiors sent Margutti to the United States was fulfilled. From a financial point of view, in his three short years Margutti sent ten thousand dollars in Mass stipends (for Masses to be celebrated), several thousand dollars in study scholarships for seminarians, and fifteen thousand dollars received

---

[8] Maestrini; op.cit., page 82.

as offerings from the mission appeals. Today that might not seem like a lot of money, but in those years the Mass stipend was five dollars in the U.S. but only 200 lire in Italy (roughly 35 cents). The stipend from one Mass in America was worth 15 Masses in Italy!

What's more, Margutti had sent several thousand dollars to his bishop in Dinajpur, Bengal, India — which became East Pakistan in 1947 and today is Bangladesh — Bishop Giovanni Battista Anselmo. Through Monsignor DeBarry, he found benefactors to finance the purchase of a large cargo boat for the mission in Macapà Brazil; and of course, he founded the American branch of the institute.

Maestrini adds,

> Considering the great contrast between the amount of wealth in this country and the heart-rending poverty of his Bengali missions and of PIME in Italy, and also the inability of the institute to do anything for them, Fr. Margutti suffered a great deal of mental anguish. But what made him suffer the most was that the PIME superiors in Italy could not send him more help so as to take advantage of the great potential for mission aid offered by this country. He felt humiliated, irritated and frustrated, but he kept on plodding along until he succeeded in the mission entrusted to him. Cardinal Mooney and Monsignor DeBarry were right in their estimation of Margutti as a great man. Indeed he was.[9]

---

[9] Maestrini; op.cit., pages 81–82.

Father Nicholas Maestrini as the new superior of PIME (1951)

The period following the departure of Fr. Margutti for Italy (October 1949) was an interval of rest before a new revival. In 1950 three new PIME Fathers came to the United States: Frs. Bruno Venturin (India), Domenico Rossi (Ethiopia, the Brazilian Amazon), and Luigi Colombo (from London). And in November of 1950, Fr. Nicholas Maestrini came for a visit. He was a born promotor, coming from his mission of Hong Kong where he had been since 1931; there he had started several printed works having to do with Chinese culture and with the apostolate of the lay people. The superior general had first sent him to open a new PIME mission in Japan and then to America in order to examine the situation and inform Rome of how things were going.

In the place of Fr. Margutti, Fr. Dante Magri was the superior of PIME in the United States; he had arrived in America at the age of 65. He was a good man and had been a good missionary in India (where he was also the chaplain of the English armed forces), but he wasn't the right person for missionary promotion and for initiating and maintaining friendships with bishops, priests, and benefactors. He didn't have any experience in the field of promotion (press, radio, conferences, mission appeals, fund-raising); he worked in an old-fashioned way with an old typewriter (which he used with only two fingers) and no secretary (since he didn't feel he needed one). Upon hearing that Fr. Maestrini was to come to the United States, he wrote him saying that there was very little work to do in the U.S.A. so it was useless for him to come to help.

But just a few months later (May 10, 1951), after Maestrini's visit, Magri wrote a letter to the superior general: "I realize that I am unable to do the work of

PIME procurator in the United States. Therefore I would be happy if you would allow me to return to India." Risso responded saying that he accepted his request and that the bishop of Hyderabad, Bishop Alfonso Beretta, was very happy to receive him back in his old mission.

On June 10, 1951, Fr. Nicholas Maestrini was named superior of PIME in the United States. The situation was the following: the institute had been entrusted with two Italian parishes (San Francesco in Detroit and Saint John the Baptist in Columbus); the headquarters of PIME was the parish rectory in Detroit, which had been enlarged with the help of Cardinal Mooney, and now contained five bedrooms.

In June 1951, there were six missionaries: four in Detroit (Dell'Agnol, Rossi, Colombo, Magri, and then Maestrini) and two in Columbus (Sala and Marrapese). Several months of the year they preached mission appeals in various dioceses, they raised funds through groups of friends gathered around our two residences. However, the institute was still unknown; there were no brochures or bulletins about PIME, and there were no promotional campaigns to make PIME's missionary activity known and to gather addresses and make friends. For many of the faithful of the two parishes entrusted to us, the PIME missionaries were simply Italian priests at their service.

Chapter II
THE GOLDEN YEARS: 1951–1956

ON JUNE 26, 1951, THE SEVEN PIME MISSIONARIES IN AMERICA met in Detroit under the new superior, Fr. Nicholas Maestrini, in order to discuss a common program of action. "The purpose of PIME's presence in the United States," they decided, "is to help the institute and its missions not only financially, but in every other possible way." This enlarged the initial plans and set the foundation for a development in America of not only one or two missionary centers, but of the very institute itself. What's more, the seven missionaries agreed to "work as a group, controlling our tendencies towards individualism, keeping alive and increasing our love and our zeal for the missions of PIME, and creating a spirit of collaboration among us."

PIME becomes international in the United States

Fr. Nicholas Maestrini had worked much in Hong Kong and China in the field of journalism and collaboration with lay movements. He therefore had a good preparation for the task of missionary development and PIME promotion which confronted him in the States. He quickly hired three assistants (a secretary, a journalist, and an office manager) with some precise programs in mind: publish brochures about the institute and a missionary magazine, write articles and send news and interviews to different newspapers, make PIME known and gather friends from outside of the limited environment of our two parishes, enter into contact with all of the diocesan directors of the Propagation of the Faith in order to offer them our collaboration in their missionary initiatives, and send letters to friends and to others whose addresses had been collected in order to invite them to collaborate in our efforts.

The meeting of June 26, 1951 signaled the turning point of our presence in America. At first we had presented ourselves as a foreign missionary institute looking for economic help. Now we were becoming an institute which recruits and forms American missionaries and has something to give to the American church — our missionary charism, diffused throughout the dioceses and parishes of the U.S. As Maestrini recounts:[1]

> PIME has a great debt of gratitude not only towards Cardinal Mooney who welcomed us, but also towards the Maryknoll missionaries who encouraged me when I went to visit them right after I arrived in America. I met, among others, Fr. John Considine, who was for Maryknoll what Frs. Manna and Tragella were for PIME. Considine told me, "If you come to America only to raise money, you will always be beggars. If you want to do something lasting in this country, accept American vocations and contribute to the growth of the American church by promoting mission and helping out in parishes and internal missions."

---

[1] In an interview on May 7, 1997, in Tequesta, Florida

American youth as missionaries in the spirit of PIME

At the beginning of the 1950s, the Catholic church in the United States was in full bloom while in Europe they were just beginning to recover from the devastating world war, and the churches of the other continents were almost non-existent in the Catholic panorama. At that time, the seminaries of the United States had almost 60,000 seminarians — more or less as many as the seminaries of the rest of the world combined! Many seminaries in Europe, especially those in the Eastern part, were either closed or under communist persecution.

The Maryknoll Missionaries, in the 1950s, were ordaining 50 to 60 new priests every year and told Fr. Maestrini that they weren't even able to scratch the surface of the potential vocations among American Catholics. There were many vocations, enough to go around for everyone, and it was providential that other missionary institutes were coming to utilize this richness for the universal mission of the church.

In 1952, Fr. Maestrini began thinking about a PIME seminary in America, in part because he realized that PIME, as long as it had no American members, would always be considered a foreign institution. He went to Cardinal Mooney, who told him, "I have seen your missionaries at work in India and Burma, and I have dreamed so much of seeing American youth formed in the spirit of PIME. Don't turn them into Italians, but make them missionaries according to your spirit." But could PIME, a secular institute (that is, without religious vows but born as a missionary expression of the Italian church) accept members of other nationalities after more than a century in which its members were only Italian?[2]

---

[2]In reality, members of other nationalities, who had come to us on their own, had been accepted individually into the institute. But no seminaries

28

To Maestrini's great surprise, Fr. Risso responded affirmatively to his proposal:

> I don't believe that there are difficulties in accepting American students in our seminaries, even if it is necessary to proceed with caution. We have to be careful not to allow ourselves to be discouraged by the difficulties involved. If other institutes are able to overcome them, why shouldn't we be able to do the same?

In November of 1951, the superior general sent this official letter:

> With regard to the seminary and the recruiting of vocations in America, we do not need any new authorization from the Congregation of Propaganda Fide because that is already contained in the letter written to Fr. Margutti on November 30, 1948. In that letter the Congregation authorized us to establish PIME in the States and to open houses with the specific purpose of recruiting vocations. We are also in line with our constitution because by opening a seminary in the States we are simply realizing a desire of our last general chapter of 1947 to become international.[3]

Thus, on October 14, 1952, three Italian theology students arrived at the Columbus, Ohio airport in order to inaugurate PIME's first seminary in America.[4] They were: Alfredo Ferronato (today a missionary in the Ama-

---

or formation houses had ever been opened outside of Italy.
[3]Maestrini; op.cit., p. 136
[4]Maestrini; op.cit., p. 150

zon), Egidio Giussani (who worked as a missionary in Hong Kong then left the institute), and Enrico Paleari (who was superior of PIME in the United States after Fr. Maestrini; he died on June 1, 1974). Soon after there were American seminarians who joined these Italians.

The friendship of Bishop Fulton J. Sheen opens many doors to PIME

The years 1951–1952 were more significant than the opening of the first seminary might indicate. They were decisive years for another reason, too. Fr. Maestrini, who was already used to the American culture and mentality, thanks to his collaboration with American missionaries in Hong Kong and China, quickly began a vast promotional campaign of PIME and its missions in order to make the institute's presence in America more visible. Even today, when talking with members of other missionary institutes and with American bishops, priests and lay people, one usually hears expressions of great admiration: "PIME has entered well into the field of mass media and missionary promotion, and you've managed to create a good image in American public opinion." This is due not only to Fr. Maestrini, but to the collaboration of PIME's confreres and PIME's many lay friends.

The expansion program that the dynamic missionary from Hong Kong wanted to implement naturally required new personnel, especially younger personnel. One of Maestrini's favorite activities in those years, of which ample traces can be found in PIME's archives in Rome, was to write impassioned letters to his superiors. He was constantly asking for personnel, complaining that those sent to him were either insufficient or just not right for the agreed upon expansion program. The superiors sent members to the States only infrequently because of negative experiences — some of the missionaries sent were not able to adapt to American life, necessitating their return to Italy or to their missions.

It must be said that, for an Italian, inculturating into the American way of life (language, food, daily rhythms, mentality, relationships with friends and family) is a lot more difficult than might be thought. A missionary who had worked in India and then the United States told me, "Notwithstanding the poverty of India and the wealth of the States, I found myself better off in India." It's not easy to explain the reason for this difficulty, but in the course of this volume, different episodes will better illustrate what I'm saying.

In 1951, PIME sent only one missionary from Italy to America, Bro. Giovanni Pillonetto. In 1952 there were seven: Frs. Antimo Boerio, James Bregola, and John Marzorati (all from China); Dante Carbonari, Rinaldo Bossi, and Gerolamo Clerici (from Burma); and Mario Venturini (from Italy). Fr. Ugo Sordo (from China) came in 1953, and in 1954 Fr. Carlo Longhini came from India, but died in a car accident after only a few months. Bro. Constantino Tranquillo Cremasco, also came from Italy. (Since his name was not common nor easy to pronounce for Americans, Fr. Maestrini rechristened him "Pius.") The presence of Brother Pius (who was born in the town of Saint Pius X) proved to be providential. He had worked in Milan in the institute's printing department, and PIME was beginning an abundant amount of publications in Detroit: the missionary magazine, postcards, PIME presentations geared towards various types of people, brochures about the missions, periodical letters to PIME's friends, donation cards in order to help those with leprosy and native catechists, advertisements, etc. And so for many years Brother Pius was PIME's printer in America (he passed

31

away in 1990). One could say that PIME was born in America thanks, in part, to his hidden labors (since he did, in fact, work in a basement!).

In the years following World War II attention to the foreign missions was alive and well in the American church. The American bishops' conference had organized its mission secretariat in Washington, D.C., which included the Society for the Propagation of the Faith, institutes and congregations with missionaries working overseas, and various lay missionary movements. One sign of the positive impact PIME was able to have on the American church was the invitation in October of 1951 from this mission secretariat for Fr. Maestrini to hold a conference on lay missionaries at the missionary convention held in Techny, Illinois.

Fulton Sheen, an auxiliary bishop of New York and the national director of the Propagation of the Faith, was present at that meeting. He had already met with Fr. Maestrini when Fr. Maestrini was looking for advice and suggestions for PIME's promotional programs. In May of 1997, a priest in New York told me that since Fulton Sheen, the American Catholic church has not had anyone so well known and influential on a national level nor anyone so much in demand in the field of mass media. This friendship with a great television personality proved to be very useful for the promotional activities which Maestrini proposed to carry out. Fulton Sheen opened many doors for us.

"We were lucky to lay down our roots in Detroit"

The years between 1951 and 1956 are fundamental for understanding PIME in America. They represent a time of new experiences, of projects and hopes, of enthusiasm and success; but they also included some disappointments and certainly, a lot of hard work. These were decisive years which gave direction to PIME in America, a direction which is followed even today: recruiting and formation of young American men for the missionary life, missionary promotion with the purpose of making friends and gathering funds for the institute's missions, pastoral work in parishes and in the home missions in New Mexico — although in the last few years these home missions have been substituted with the mission among the Mixtec Indians in Mexico and by the Chinese parish in Toronto, Canada.

The first monthly bulletin for PIME's friends, entitled *Sts. Peter and Paul Missionary Bulletin* — with the subtitle, *Love and Service* — came out in January of 1952: 1,000 copies in January, 2,500 in March, 5,500 in June. Fr. Maestrini attributes the success of the bulletin to the fact that PIME was able to adapt itself to the American ecclesiastical environment. It was popular because of the simplicity and freshness of the missionaries' letters, which Miss Joyce Daigue, the journalist hired to work for PIME's publications office, translated and "americanized."

The activities of missionary promotion helped make new friends: parish mission appeals preached by all the Fathers, participation in the missionary displays organized by the Propagation of the Faith Society in different dioceses and cities, articles in Catholic newspapers, and the new initiatives which Fr. Maestrini began in order to make the institute well known, such as the Knights of Charity Dinner and PIME Golf Day.

But, Maestrini adds,

> The cordial support of Cardinal Mooney and of Monsignor DeBarry, diocesan director of the Propagation of the Faith, helped us a lot, as did the fact that we established

ourselves in Detroit. If we had gone to New York, Chicago, or Los Angeles, we would have been lost among many orders and congregations. In Detroit we emerged right away because we were unique — there were no other missionary institutes; our initiatives showed up in the local papers and then the national ones, on the radio, and on television. The heads of Ford, Chrysler, General Motors, and other important companies and institutions would eat supper at our house. Detroit is a big city, but these were events that made news even on a national level. By now PIME in the Detroit area (around five million inhabitants) is an institution known and praised by all. This would have been unthinkable if we were in New York.

Maestrini continues,

There were two important moments in this publicity campaign at the beginning of the 1950s, which contributed to PIME's renown. The first was when a local newspaper published some news about PIME and wrote, "Just as the world moves on Detroit's wheels, so the missionaries formed by PIME in Detroit will carry to the human masses help which will liberate them from their misery, and spiritual values which come from the knowledge of God's love." This became like a slogan, which went around in the media. Another time we asked some of our friends to publish some articles and advertisements about PIME in newspapers and on the radio since we weren't able to spend any money on publicity. One of our friends was even able to have an article about PIME and its Foster Parents program published in *Reader's Digest*, which sold more than seven million copies! We received thousands of letters, offerings, and subscriptions to our bulletin.

Not fund-raising, but friend-raising

In the beautiful book in which he describes his mission in Hong Kong,[5] Fr. Maestrini dedicates ample space to one of the most interesting experiences of those years: the formation of lay Catholics and collaboration with them, giving them responsibility in the institution of the church. In the twenty years that he worked in China (1931–1951), Maestrini distinguished himself as a missionary with apostolic spirit and an ability for groundbreaking and successful activity, above all in the fields of journalism, culture, and the lay apostolate.

In Hong Kong, he founded the Catholic Centre (headquarters for the diocese's journalism and lay apostolate activities), the Catholic Truth Society (a publishing house), and the Sunday Examiner (Hong Kong's weekly Catholic newspaper). He continued the prestigious monthly China Missionary Bulletin which moved from Shanghai in 1948 due to the Communist occupation of the city. He encouraged the formation of Catholic writers, among them the famous Dr. John Wu,

---

[5]*China: Lost Mission?* PIME World Press, Detroit 1992.

China's ambassador to the Holy See.[6] He collaborated in the growth of lay associations and movements such as Catholic Action , the Legion of Mary, and the Grail. He initiated Catholic youth and student groups and the Chinese Businessmen's Catholic Club.

PIME developed itself in America on the basis of this same spirit: dynamism, formation and collaboration with the laity, inculturation and openness to American society in its various expressions. This is a common tendency in the church today, which is overcoming its formalism and clericalism. But in the first half of the 1950s it was a revolutionary approach which was not common in the ecclesiastical environment, especially in Italy; the difficulties which Maestrini found in PIME often came from this different cultural vision and apostolic approach. Maestrini's principle, which he declared many times, is: "Not fund-raising, but friends-raising". "My concept," says Maestrini today, "wasn't to find economic help, but to enlarge the circle of friends of the missions, of prayer, of vocations, of collaboration in our initiatives; the money would follow as a consequence."

How does one find new friends? Ads in newspapers can help, but the personal touch is the most important. Fr. Maestrini, with the help of dedicated and able friends, initiated the Knights of Charity Dinner and the PIME Golf Day. These events have since become institutions for PIME and have been imitated by other religious congregations and dioceses.

Says Fr. Maestrini today,

> What we accomplished in the early 1950s,
> we really owe to the lay people with which I

---

[6] Doctor John Wu is the author of a famous book on the spirituality of Saint Theresa of the Child Jesus: *The Science of Love, A Chinese Intellectual Encounters Therese of Lisieux*, PIME, Milan 1997, 126 pages.

surrounded myself, the daily collaborators of the in-house staff I created, and those friends who readily offered themselves and their help when we truly needed it. At that time the general directorate said I was going too fast and they tried to slow me down. But I've never done anything without the written approval of my superiors (naturally, I would explain and insist until they gave me that approval). There must be pounds and pounds of my letters in PIME's archives in Rome. I needed to explain everything several times in order to make them understand that certain steps were unavoidable if we wanted to move ahead. Otherwise we would just be creating a stunted presence of PIME, closed in its little yard of two parishes and an office just to raise a little money.

We remained too Italian

After the original founding period of Fr. Margutti, PIME in America entered the phase of the "great leap forward" (no reference intended to the "leap forward" which Mao Tse Tung attempted several years later in China). In just a few years (1951–1956), practically everything was established, and in the following years it became a matter of maintaining the activities (or cancelling some due to the shortage of personnel): seminaries in Ohio, Michigan and New Jersey; the mission magazine; the promotional center and its initiatives; the mission in New Mexico; the acquisition or gifts of land, and construction.

Maestrini today admits that he made some mistakes in his eagerness to carry out a plan which was, for him, very clear and exciting, though not agreed upon by many of the other Fathers with whom he collaborated.

He told me the following in an interview:[7]

> I understood America, and I had many contacts with American bishops, priests, and missionaries who encouraged me to move ahead in that direction. Other PIME missionaries who were with me didn't understand America and had few outside contacts. I asked for advice from people who knew more about America than I (that is, from American religious and American lay friends), not from those who knew less than I (my Italian confreres). I asked them to follow me and to have faith. This was a mistake: I followed my plans more than I followed the growth stages of my confreres. For this reason I was never very popular among the Fathers here in America; I went too fast. My idea was to build up our seminaries and give an economic and promotional base to the institute in ten or fifteen years. Then, I thought, I would retire and act as a spiritual director for our seminarians, helping to form them in the spirit of PIME. But when I finally retired at the beginning of the 1970s, there were no more seminarians.

In a report prepared for PIME's general chapter in 1965,[8] Fr. Lorenzo Chiesa, who was then the rector of PIME's high-school seminary in Newark, Ohio, discuss-

---

[7]Tequesta, Florida on May 7–8, 1997.
[8]"*Riflessioni e osservazioni sull'internazionalizzazione*", in *Il Vincolo*, 1965, special issue *"In attesa del Capitolo 1965, Raccolta di studi e relazioni,"* pages 60–64.

es the internationalization of the institute, above all from the point of view of theological and historical motivations. He concludes by saying that while a precise, positive conviction in this regard has not yet been reached in PIME, the process of internationalization is moving ahead anyway. Seminaries are being opened; we find ourselves facing an already existing reality; we work in a spirit of obedience "in an undertaking that most people don't completely understand, without even the appearance of being asked our opinion before being involved in it." Fr. Chiesa wasn't really talking about internationality per se, since this was a decision already made in the United States and in Brazil, but was only affirming that this conviction needed to take root in everyone before jumping fully into this undertaking.

Fr. Casto Marrapese told me,[9]

> Fr. Maestrini was marvelous, a great mover and shaker, and able to visualize even the most difficult dreams, but we were all different from him. We had been in America only a short time and we realized that there were huge differences between American and Italian ways. We spoke with other institutes and they all told us of the enormous difficulties for an Italian to educate young Americans. I've worked a lot and I believe that I did pretty well in both Columbus and out East, and I can truly say that I really like America. But it's one thing to make friends, plan publicity initiatives, find funds, construct seminaries, be a parish priest, and all the other activities which we

---

[9]Interviewed in Newark on May 13, 1997.

manage to do well in; it's another thing to form a young American, who comes from a completely different culture, mentality, language, tradition, church, and Christian lifestyle, into a missionary with our spirit. We have problems doing it in Italy, so imagine the difficulties in America!

Looking back, Fr. Maestrini says,

I believe that our growth was blessed by God and all of those who saw us from the outside used to say the same thing. Our first seminary here was built in 1952, but in 1969, when I stepped down as director of the US region, we had around 120 students in our seminaries: 80 on the high-school level and 40 on the college/theology level. At Maryglade Seminary we had all the classes up to the last year of theology taught by professors with doctorates. Our educational program was recognized by the state and we were affiliated with the Catholic University of America in Washington D.C.

We were hit by the church's vocation crisis at a very delicate moment, and we also suffered because we generally remained too Italian; many of us didn't really adapt well to the life, language, culture, and mentality of America.

Our missionaries have an excellent spirit

Is an Italian institute, consisting of Italian missionaries and with an Italian tradition, able to form American priests and missionaries? This question was discussed at great length inside of PIME with both positive and negative responses. In fact, PIME was born in Saronno, Italy in 1850 as the Lombard Seminary for the Foreign Missions. It was founded by Monsignor Angelo Ramazzotti (who then went on to become bishop of Pavia and then Patriarch of Venice) upon Pius IX's wish and in the name of the Lombard bishops in order to send diocesan priests to the missions. It has always presented itself as the expression of the Italian dioceses and church, and in the past it considered internationalization as something more appropriate to a religious congregation than to an institute of Italian diocesan priests.

I asked the "internationality question" to some American PIME confreres, and they gave me answers based not upon theory but upon their life experience in PIME. As Fr. Edward Miley recounts,

> In the 1950s, when I entered the institute, I liked PIME because it entered quickly and immediately into the mainstream of the American church and American society. Ten years after its first missionary, Fr. Guido Margutti, came here, our institute already had two seminaries, three residences, two parishes, a magazine, a missionary promotion center with many interesting initiatives for the American church, and a home mission in New Mexico.
>
> Other institutes, even some larger than PIME, entered the mainstream much more slowly precisely due to the difficulties of the American environment. Or else they had planted themselves here at the end of the last century or beginning of this one when the American church was less organized and less mature. We, on the other hand,

41

came right after the Second World War from a defeated and unappreciated country, at a time when the American church was full of vitality and many vocations and didn't feel the need for foreign priests. PIME contributed with an open spirit to the American church in the area of promoting mission and in stimulating vocations. It broke the ice of a dead-end situation (everyone for himself) by collaborating from the very beginning with the dioceses, the Maryknoll missionaries, and Propagation of the Faith, while other institutes tended to remain closed in their own little activities.

I believe that the decision PIME made which had the most influence on ecclesiastical public opinion in the first half of the 1950s was to take on the home mission in New Mexico. With the scarce number of personnel available, we immediately sent four missionaries to begin a difficult mission in one of the most isolated and religiously abandoned territories of our country.

All of this deals with the spirit and missionary tradition of PIME. But I repeated the question to Fr. Miley: is our institute adapted to forming American priests and missionaries? Ed smiled and responded,

I think that's a silly question. I believe that our missionaries have an excellent spirit expressed in, for example, the lives of Fr. Tulio Favali and Fr. Salvatore Carzedda. They were two young missionaries that I met and knew here in the United States and who were then killed in the Philippines while witnessing to the love of Christ, one in 1985 and the other in 1992. Two martyrs for faith and love. That is what counts: we have to present the lives of missionaries like them, who are models able to form even today's youth. The rest the Lord takes care of.

Yes, but after fifty years of presence in the United States, PIME has only twelve American priests. Many others have left the institute, being incardinated into U.S. dioceses or else leaving the priesthood. Fr. Miley continues,

I believe that the reason for this in some cases is that different American fathers didn't really understand well the struggles involved in adapting to a difficult world such as that of the missions. They went to the missions and quickly returned to America since they hadn't been able to adapt themselves. Returning to America, they went back to their dioceses in order to do some pastoral work. Some have left the priesthood, it's true, but that's something common to every diocese and in every institute. But the better part of those who left PIME are still priests in their dioceses and remain good friends with PIME; I don't know any of them who are against PIME.

I'm optimistic about the future of PIME in the States

Fr. Ken Mazur, missionary in Japan for the last seven years, adds,

We Americans in Japan are strangers twice: first because the Japanese world that surrounds us is so different from ours in everything; and secondly, because in our mission houses there's an Italian environment: the food is Italian, the language used is Italian, there are lively discussions about Italian politics and sports. But the situation is changing, both because PIME is truly becoming international, in terms of a common mentality and style of life, and because now we all go to Italy and learn Italian. Actually, my Italian has improved in Japan, because that is the only way to speak with my confreres; we don't use Japanese with one another, nor even English, which everyone has studied.

Fr. Sandy Garzarelli was PIME's first American priest. His story is both interesting and symbolic:

During and after the last world war I was, beginning in 1944, in the U.S. Navy. In the summer of 1945 I was in Okinawa and I participated in the last heavy battles of the war. In September of 1945 I was in Hong Kong, where I returned years later as a PIME missionary. Then I was in Shanghai and on the border of Korea where I worked, as an American soldier, with the Chinese nationalist army. So I'd had an adventurous life in the Orient which opened the world's horizons to me.

And so, returning after having finished my service in the military, I wanted to become a missionary and a priest. I did odd jobs, including two years as a professional dancer, and then I went to the Maryknoll Missionaries who at that time had huge numbers of vocations from the young Americans returning from the war. The Maryknoll vocation director, who had to choose from among all of the applicants, told me, "You're not right for us." I returned home to Philadelphia very disappointed, but I absolutely wanted to become a priest. My pastor told me to join the diocesan seminary; but I knew that I wanted to be a missionary.

So, in 1954 my pastor sent me to PIME where, in 1961, I became the institute's first American priest. I always felt comfortable with PIME and I love PIME for its spirit, for the many missionaries that I met who were always a good example for me, and for the freedom and sense of giving that pervades the community. While I was a young student at PIME's seminaries in Newark, Armada, and Maryglade, I saw other American students around me who resented some of the conditions we lived in. For example, the Fathers spoke Italian among themselves, the food was more Italian than American, they made us study the Italian language, etc. I never truly suffered on account of these things; I adapted myself and I liked the lifestyle of the PIME missionaries. Maybe it's because I'm from Italian descent and I like Italy.

In 1963 I left for Hong Kong and it was there that I found difficulty with the language, the Chinese lifestyle, the climate, etc. In 1963 I was 37 years old (I was born in 1926); maybe that's an age in which it isn't easy to adapt oneself to China. But I was comfortable with the environment within PIME in Hong Kong and I left many friends there. I returned to America in 1969 and I was assigned to do administrative work. Then I asked PIME to allow me to return to my diocese of Philadelphia, where I've been for the last 25 years, first as an associate and then 12 years as pastor. But I've always kept good contact with the institute and several of its priests.

During that time, homesickness for the missionary lifestyle was growing in me and I asked PIME if they would still want to send me to the missions. When I received a positive response I went to my archbishop telling him that I wanted to return to the missions. The bishop proposed that I go with the diocese; some of our diocese's priests are in Latin America and I could have joined up with them. But I preferred to work with PIME, and now I'm an associate member of the institute. I worked for 18 months in PIME's missions in India, and then the government wouldn't renew my visa anymore; now I'm leaving for Papua New Guinea to work with the bishop of Vanimo, Cesare Bonivento, a PIME member.

I am really happy to share this experience of my great joy in being able to be in PIME once more. It seems to me that the institute is doing that right thing in becoming international. You have an excellent missionary spirit and a beautiful tradition of work in the missions; these are charismatic riches that you can't just keep for yourselves, but that you must communicate to the other churches. The difficulties that you encounter in America are many, foremost the language. But this is a challenge for any missionary institute. If you've confronted this challenge so courageously in China, India, Japan, Bangladesh, Africa, Thailand, Cambodia, Brazil, and so on, why not in America, too? Today vocations have gone down for everyone, but I'm optimistic about the future of PIME in the States.

CHAPTER III

THE GREAT ADVENTURE OF FORMING AMERICAN MISSIONARIES

THE HISTORY OF PIME SEMINARIES IN AMERICA IN NO WAY DIF-fers from that of the institute's seminaries in Italy and Brazil. It's a continuous series of openings and closings, a frequent change of superiors and formation directors, and a pattern of hopes and disappointments. The last thirty years have been difficult for the entire church especially in the field of vocations to the priesthood and religious life.

Decline in vocations for the entire Western church

The United States is no exception. The American Catholic church has seen the following decline in numbers from 1965 to 1995:[1]

	1965	1995
Bishops	140	290
Priests (both diocesan and religious)	58,132	49,551
New priests ordained	994	522
Permanent deacons	—	11,452
Theology seminarians	8,325	3,177
Religious brothers	12,271	6,578
Religious sisters	179,954	92,107
Parishes	17,637	19,723
Parishes without a resident priest	549	2,161
Catholics	45,640,619	60,190,605
(% of population)	(24%)	(23.2%)

---

[1] The data which follow are taken from *The CARA Report: Research on American Catholics and the U.S. Catholic Church*, published by the Center

Visiting the United States and talking with various persons in the ecclesiastical sphere, even today one hears unsettling news. In the 1950s it was rare, and constituted a public scandal which made headlines in all the newspapers, if a priest left the priesthood. Today it has become so common that it doesn't even make news (unless there are worse elements involved).

The history of American vocations to PIME needs to be read in this frame of a generational crisis which certainly, due to the action of the Holy Spirit, will see a positive outcome when God wills it. God knows how to produce good even in the worst of situations. We must wait with faith. This is the hope and optimism which I found visiting and interviewing our missionaries in the United States, and above all the American fathers of PIME.

Seven PIME seminaries in the United States

The first PIME seminary was opened on October 14, 1953 in Columbus with three Italian seminarians sent to the States to study English and theology. It was officially inaugurated by Bishop Michael J. Ready on December 4, 1952 in a house in the residential neighborhood of East North Broadway in Columbus. Fr. Dominic Rossi was the first rector and Fr. Casto Marrapese was the treasurer. They were together with three Italian theology seminarians who were studying at the Josephinum (a theological seminary of German origin), and two Americans who were in the college program in Columbus (19 and 21 years old). It was the modest but decisive beginning of a long journey.

for Applied Research in the Apostolate (CARA), Georgetown University, Washington, 1996. The number of bishops comes from the *1996 Official Catholic Directory*.

At the end of the 1950s, after the institute's general chapter in 1957, PIME, which had come to the States looking for aid to send to the missions and to the institute in Italy, took up the task of recruiting and forming missionary vocations as its primary purpose.

As was happening in Italy in the 1950s and 1960s, the construction of new seminaries became the most relevant external manifestation of PIME in America. Up to the end of the 1960s, the growing number of vocations brought about the construction of big buildings for big communities. Then the decline began, which in the 1970s and 1980s saw a drastic reduction in the number of youth wishing to become priests, and forced the sale or remodeling of those big buildings for different uses.

Father Maestrini, in his book celebrating the first 25 years of PIME in America,[2] recounts each step of the labors involved in constructing or acquiring the seven seminaries which PIME has had in the United States:

- Columbus, Ohio: theology and college (1952–1956).
- Newark Ohio: high school (opened in 1956; the seminary closed in 1990, and the facility is now used as a missionary promotion, retreat, and meeting center).
- Armada, Michigan: year of formation, novitiate (1958–1963).
- Maryglade in Memphis, Michigan: college (1960–1972), theology (1960–1961).
- Oakland, New Jersey: high school (1961–1972), and theology (1961–1976).
- Chicago, Illinois: theology (1976–1995; beginning in 1996 the American students have gone to PIME's in-

---

[2] *P.I.M.E. in the United States, The First Twenty-Five Years, 1947–1972*, PIME World Press, Detroit 1994, 354 pages.

ternational theologate in Monza, Italy).

- Detroit, Michigan: college (opened in 1972, and still continues as College Formation Community, with classes at the nearby University of Detroit Mercy).

Behind this simple list it is easy to understand the amount of work and money — from American benefactors and from the priestly ministry of our fathers — which the PIME missionaries in America have spent for acquiring land, planning the seminaries, and the construction and furnishing of these buildings. Besides the seminaries listed here, we shouldn't forget PIME's other residences: the regional house in Detroit which has had three locations (from East Boston Boulevard in the beginning, to Oakland Avenue in 1966, and finally to Quincy Ave. in 1974, where it remains today); the mission promotion center which was first in Detroit, then Fraser, Michigan (1974–1995), and then again in Detroit, sharing the regional house building; the residence in Tequesta, Florida (from 1974 to the present); the parish and mission center in Los Angeles; a small house in Wayne, New Jersey to replace the large Oakland property (sold in 1995); and the maintenance of the home missions in New Mexico.

In the report given to the 1971 general chapter of PIME, at the height of PIME's vocation boom in America, Fr. Henry Paleari, then regional superior, painted a very positive picture of the institute's 25 years in this country, above all in the work of founding and operating seminaries, residences, and parishes. In that itemized report,[3] Fr. Paleari praises "the fathers and brothers who are very involved in and dedicated to their work, who fulfill their duties with responsibility and ad-

---

[3] Enrico Paleari, *"Relazioni per il Capitolo 1971"*, page 26.

equate preparation. Around two-thirds are working in recruiting, formation, and administration for the seminaries." At that time, there were 38 PIME members in the United States.

Fr. Nicholas Maestrini, upon the occasion of that same 1971 chapter, prepared his own report which reads,

> In a period of just 15 years (1955–1969) our American friends have contributed — just for the construction of seminaries — some three million dollars. There are tens of thousands of persons who have contributed with a true spirit of sacrifice because they believed in our promise to form American priests for the missions.[4]

38 American priests ordained by PIME

In 50 years, more than one thousand students have passed through PIME's seminaries in the United States. PIME's alumni association, born in the 1960s and now being reestablished in earnest, has nearly 800 addresses of friends, many of whom are important professionals, people who have done well in society, as well as priests in American dioceses.

In all, PIME has ordained 38 American priests, of which:

- one died as a member of PIME in 1978 (Fr. Charles Minck, who was regional superior from 1973 to 1977);
- eleven are still members of PIME: three in Japan, one in India, one in Bangladesh, one in Papua New Guinea, one in the Brazilian Amazon, one studying

---

[4] "Pro-memoria per i membri del Capitolo del PIME del 1971".

in Rome, and three in the United States (one of whom is preparing to leave for the missions);

- one who is today a PIME "associate" working as a missionary in Papua New Guinea (Fr. Sandy Garzarelli);
- 24 who have left PIME, eleven after an experience in the missions; of these 24, 12 remain in active priestly ministry;
- there was also one American PIME Brother, who has left the community.

It may seem a poor total for 50 years of work promoting mission, stimulating vocations and forming students in the seminaries. It would be if these were normal times. But looking at the last half century of the church's life, who could say that the times have been "normal"?

The number one problem: finding the right personnel

In his report to the 1971 chapter (already cited), Fr. Paleari wrote of the difficulty in recruiting vocations:

> In our first years adult vocations were accepted for college and theology. Publicity was done in the press. Beginning in 1957 we also began looking for vocations for the minor seminary (high school) using recruiters just for that. The biggest difficulty for the superiors of the United States lies in finding fathers who are willing to be vocation recruiters. Many think they don't have the extraordinary capacities which would be needed since this is the most difficult task in America, just as in Italy. Now we have two recruiters and soon a third will be added, an American who was or-

dained just this year.

Still, Fr. Maestrini points out that even with all the difficulties, vocations remained the top priority:

> There were many more vocational directors at work from 1955–1969 than at any other time. The task of the mission center, both under my tenure and that of Paleari, was to assist the vocational directors with the printing of brochures, folders and clerical work, etc.

In the history of PIME in America, finding the right person for vocation recruiting, for working in the seminaries, and for formation has always been difficult. PIME's general archives in Rome contain numerous letters from the superiors in Detroit to the general directorate dealing with personnel. There were never enough people to do the job, and finding trained and capable replacements to allow others to return to the missions was a continual concern of the Detroit superiors.

PIME's real problem, in Italy and Brazil just as in the United States, is that we are a missionary institute made up of non-religious; our members enter PIME to go to the missions and only reluctantly accept positions within the institute's structures. In addition, the superiors are concerned about sending everybody to the missions as soon as possible so that they can adapt to the difficult missionary lifestyle without losing the institute's spirit (by having remained too long in their own country).

And so it happens that, even when someone is found who is able and prepared for a certain formation or missionary promotion job, it's rare that he remains for a long time in that position because of his understandable desire to go or to return to the mission field.

As a result the placement and continuity of truly capable and expert personnel remains difficult. At the same time, some of those who come to America after a certain age, after a long experience in the missions, find it difficult to adjust fully to their new work.

Presently, for the work of stimulating vocations in the immense expanse of North America, there is only one missionary in charge of following the youth who express a desire to become missionaries: Fr. Claudio Corti, a thirty-year-old Italian priest who arrived in the States right after his ordination in 1992. He is the first father in the last fifteen years to be sent from Italy to the States right after ordination. He loves his work; he has learned English quite well and in just five years has inculturated himself well for his work with American youth. But he has already been assigned a mission destination and will leave in 1998, just when he could begin to see the fruits of his service.

It is right for him to graduate to mission *ad gentes.* It is why he was ordained a PIME priest. After experiencing mission life he will become an even more effective messenger and will gain credibility as a missioner.

Well prepared formation directors and teachers, but then no students!

For this reason, as Fr. Maestrini understood from the very beginning, missionaries — even more so than priests from dioceses or religious orders — need to be helped by collaborators and lay friends; we can't do it alone.

This is true also for the education of students in our seminaries. In the 1950s and 1960s, PIME tried to take care of its own formation structures in America, including its own teachers. Some thirty Italian missionaries studied in both religious and secular American universities, getting their bachelors and masters degrees in various specializations, always with a great spirit of sacrifice. In the 1960s our schools at Maryglade, in Newark and in Oakland were standing on their own with degreed professors, libraries, museums, and teaching tools of every type.

The hard work succeeded and the most beautiful example of the success was Maryglade Seminary in Memphis, Michigan. It was affiliated with the Catholic University of Washington and could grant bachelor's and master's degrees for college and theology. The maximum number of students was 45 during the 1964–65 academic year. The following year the ten theology students went to the Josephinum in Columbus (living at our seminary in Newark, Ohio) and then to the Darlington Diocesan Seminary in 1968 (living in PIME's seminary in Oakland, New Jersey).

Visiting the grounds of the former Maryglade today, one is moved by the grandness and beauty of the campus: the large missionary mosaic covering the entire front wall of the chapel, the surrounding park, the ball fields, the lake, etc. The seminary, which could host a total of 110 students, was closed and sold in 1972 when there were only 19 college students.[5].

The adventure involved in constructing and operating Maryglade is a grandiose epic, and Fr. Maestrini rightly dedicates many pages to it in his book on PIME's first 25 years in America.[6] In the 1950s, priesthood and missionary vocations were continually growing in the United States; it didn't seem out of place to build a

---

[5] In 1974–1975, the college program moved to Detroit with 40 students.
[6] Three Chapters: "The Maryglade Story", "The Growth of Maryglade", "The End of Maryglade", pages 251–286; in *P.I.M.E. in the United States, The First Twenty-Five Years, 1947–1972*, PIME World Press, Detroit, 1994.

large campus. This is all the more true because, from the middle of the 1950s, many dedicated and hard-working friends were becoming attached to the community of PIME. We needed to propose a high aim for them to reach. As it was conceived in the beginning, understood within the American climate of the 1950s, it was exalting.

Unfortunately, when the construction was finished, when the teachers were prepared with the necessary academic degrees, when the debts were paid, the library was completed and the building was furnished, the only thing missing were the students! PIME experienced the same thing in Italy with the construction (or renovation) of big seminaries in the 1950s and 1960s, which today have all been sold or rented out.

The construction of Maryglade

The Maryglade story is worthy of being told because it is a great example of the spirit which PIME brought to America. The initiative began with Mr. John Gardella, an accomplished businessman in Detroit who was, in the 1950s, president of the PIME Friends Committee.

Knowing that PIME was looking for a property on which to build its college and theology, Gardella set himself in motion with other friends. He presented three possible properties for sale near Detroit to Fr. Maestrini, assuring him the financial support of the association. The plans for the land and the seminary were shown to Cardinal Edward Mooney, archbishop of Detroit, who told Maestrini that he would prefer that they buy the land in Macomb County — the only county in the diocese that still did not have any religious institution. In this way, the missionaries would be able to help out in the nearby parishes.

Memphis was the property farthest from Detroit (60

miles), but it was bought to help out the diocese. The property, made up of 127 acres — half cultivated as farm land and half covered with woods, was bought with a 10,000 dollar loan given by the PIME Friends Committee (the cost of the land was 27,000 dollars). Mr. George Gardella (John's uncle) paid off the cost of the land as a donation made in gratitude to the Blessed Mother for the recovery of his wife, Rose, from a severe illness.

It was in this way that the Maryglade adventure began. The question of fund-raising wasn't easy, given the urgency of building Maryglade. In fact, the 1957 general assembly of PIME in Rome (the land was bought in April, the assembly was held in September and October) had decided to make the recruiting and formation of new missionaries its number one priority in America. Since the seminaries in Newark and Armada just weren't big enough for all of the students, a big fund-raising campaign was started in 1958–59. At the kickoff luncheon for the campaign — in which George Gardella was given the title of "Knight of Charity" — more than 500 people representing the cream of the industrial and financial world in Detroit participated.

The campaign for raising 100,000 dollars was carried out by the building committee, which was made up of a group of faithful friends. After having prepared bulletins and brochures, the first part of the campaign, begun in 1959, was quickly able to raise half of the total cost: 50,000 dollars, a tidy sum in 1959. The second part of the campaign was less fruitful, but it enlarged the circle of friends and benefactors. The total cost of more than a million dollars for construction and furnishings was then covered with donations and campaigns, bank loans, and by friends who lent money without interest.

PIME Bishop Giuseppe Obert, bishop of Dinajpur

(Bangladesh), blessed the cornerstone on May 22, 1960. In September of that same year, Maryglade opened its doors to eight priest-professors, two lay professors, and 22 college and theology students. The blessing of the new seminary was done by Egidio Vagnozzi, the apostolic delegate to the United States, on May 18, 1961. Three sisters of the Missionaries of the Immaculate worked side by side with the PIME missionaries at Maryglade beginning in 1959[7].

The spirit of Maryglade lives on

Fr. Maestrini writes,[8]

> Maryglade as a complex of buildings has been sold but the spirit of Maryglade lives on and is prophetic for indicating the future. Maryglade was not merely a construction block. It was and still is a living spirit of partnership between businessmen, common people, and us PIME missionaries in the great spiritual and humanitarian work of bringing the knowledge of God to non-Christian nations and alleviating their physical and spiritual poverty. Perhaps in no other part of the United States was a major seminary ever built with the financial collaboration of members of all major American faiths: Catholic, Protestant, and Jew. This collaboration did not consist only

[7] The Missionaries of the Immaculate were founded by PIME's superior general, Bishop Lorenzo Maria Balconi, in Milan in 1936. They worked with the PIME Missionaries in India, Bangladesh, Hong Kong, Brazil, the Amazon, Guinea-Bissau, Cameroun, the Philippines, and Papua New Guinea. They worked in the United States at Maryglade from 1959–1972. After the seminary closed they returned to Italy.
[8] Maestrini; op.cit., p. 284.

of the collection of funds; it constituted also a relationship of love and collaboration on the part of all.

Maestrini then goes on to explain the spirit of Maryglade.

Our major seminary in the United States was founded with the slogan: "Just as the world moves on Detroit's wheels, so the missionaries formed by PIME in Detroit will carry to the human masses help which will liberate them from their misery, and spiritual values which come from the knowledge of God's love."

The Maryglade board of trustees was made up of lay Catholics, Protestants and Jews. The very idea of a higher institute of mission formation followed by the actual construction of Maryglade came about in an ecumenical spirit of collaboration. This was the spirit of Maryglade which PIME was able, through the work of Fr. Maestrini and his priest and lay collaborators, to bring to the attention of the American society and the American church. The success of this operation was friendship: "Not fund-raising, but friend-raising."

"Friendship is the key to success," writes Fr. Maestrini.

We believed that even the smallest donation given to us for the missions was the beginning of a friendship, not a mere exchange of alms for prayers. From the very beginning of our promotion work in Detroit, we emphasized to our students that we were not fund-raisers merely interested in collecting money for the missions and the needs of the institute, but we were here to make friends for the missions, to educate them in the missionary ideal, to make partners who would collaborate with us in the work of evangelization to the non-Christians.

The difficult issue of theology

From the 1970s onwards things got difficult, in America as in Brazil and Italy, in the operation of a seminary and assuring that the students received an education in line with church teachings. There were many distractions, too many disagreements, a certain anti-Roman spirit, and a theology which was forever searching and wasn't giving the support of a firm and serene faith.

In PIME's archives in Rome, letters and reports can be found in which the PIME fathers express dissatisfaction about the theological teaching being given in the schools that our students were attending. Naturally, there are different thoughts about this. For example, Fr. Amedeo Barbieri[9] affirms that the theological school of Darlington, other than maybe in the case of two or three professors out of thirty, was sound and orthodox. He considers the move from of our theologate from Darlington to Catholic Theological Union in Chicago, as "a wrong and hurried decision, made without even consulting one PIME member like me." But this is only one example to show how, in those years, it was difficult even for the superiors to judge and decide on matters so delicate as the teaching of theology — a decisive fac-

---

[9] Fr. Amedeo Barbieri taught sacred Scripture in American seminaries in two periods (1959–1965 and 1971–1983), with a brief intermission in Hong Kong. I interviewed him in Milan on June 23, 1997.

tor in the education of the seminarians.

In Fr. Barbieri's opinion, the difficulties of the early times in the formation of American students came above all from the mediocre quality of those who were entering the seminaries: adult vocations who were ex-soldiers and youth who hadn't been accepted by the diocesan seminaries.

> We readily took everybody in order to fill our seminaries. But it was the wrong policy to follow, because it lowered expectations; in fact, almost nobody managed to reach ordination to the priesthood. Then, after Vatican Council II the vocation crisis began and unorthodox theological teaching became more prevalent.

> On the other hand, even constructing Maryglade when we had so few students was a mistake — we young teachers were against it — because it concentrated the attention of the American region of PIME on the external considerations of construction, publicity and finances while those of us in the seminary were lacking both sufficiently mature students and adequate formation methods for America. Even in Italy, in the 1950s and 1960s, we built big seminaries which then turned out to be useless. But we had hundreds of students, over 250 students in Italy in 1960 with 70 in theology, and PIME had a stability there which it had gained with a century of history. In America we were still at the beginning, with few students and without any formation experience. We don't need to feel too guilty, though, because the other Italian mission-

ary institutes, who didn't have the genius of Fr. Maestrini in public relations and who began in a more modest way than we, didn't have any better results than we did.

"The seminaries must form priests, not simply gentlemen"

Fr. Carlo Brivio spent many years in America (1961–1985) working in the theology and college programs; he was also rector. Today he teaches in the theological seminary in Monza, Italy. He comments on the theme of the seminaries.

> I have always been in favor of internationalization. I always felt that PIME needed to open itself up and not stay just Italian because, in today's world, that would be absurd for a missionary institute. But working many years in the seminaries I realized the difficulties that we face in forming American youth in our spirit. Americans have great qualities: a practical, precise, and organized spirit, as well as generosity and efficiency. But the spiritual life in general is very superficial; that's just how they are. It's in their culture and in their mentality, and you can't do anything about it. But every once in a while you find an exception.
>
> I often asked myself the same question: what is there to do? Maybe the answer will come with time as we, as an institute, integrate ourselves into the American culture and learn to listen, to understand, and to explain ourselves to our American youth. But we need to stand strong on the foundation of spirituality and prayer. We can't

allow ourselves to fall into the superficiality of certain American seminaries whose goal seems to be to form gentlemen, rather than priests.

I admire America, its people, and its church, but we can not allow ourselves to be so overcome by this feeling to the point of losing our identity and formation. Otherwise you can no longer give your contribution to their spiritual and missionary growth.

We have to admit that up to now we haven't been able to bring a true missionary spirit to America nor to create an environment of an authentic spirit of prayer and mission in our seminaries, as Fr. Paolo Manna wanted.[10] We let ourselves get caught up in the constructions, money, external advertising, and organization. The American way, if you don't go against the flow, carries you towards these priorities. I'm not judging the people; in fact I believe that our missionaries in America, especially those who were already more mature with mission experience when they came, have given and continue to give a good example. But all of us together haven't been able to give a missionary and spiritual basis to the institute and its seminaries. On one hand it's true that we're still too

---

[10] Fr. Paolo Manna (1872–1952), missionary in Burma and then director of PIME's magazine *Le Missioni Cattoliche* (today *Mondo e Missione*), was general superior of the institute from 1924 to 1934. In his circular letters to the membership he gave a clear and articulate description of the missionary spirituality which represents the tradition of PIME. The formation personnel in the institute's seminaries all look to him for inspiration.

Italian (we speak Italian in our different communities, we eat Italian food, etc.), but on the other hand maybe we've become too Americanized as well.

The contrast between promotion and seminary formation

Thus, in the past, one could note a type of schizophrenia in the U.S. region of PIME, which has by now been overcome. Maybe it was the price to pay for a fortuitous and tumultuous growth in just a few short years, a growth which was neither understood nor easily accepted by an institute which up to that time had been only Italian. But it was a providential growth in the sense that it gave a positive image of the institute to the American society and church, and a promotional and economic base on which it rests even up to the present.

The stories of Fr. Barbieri and Fr. Brivio tell of the suffering of many missionaries dedicated to the formation of American youth, dedicated to helping them become priests and missionaries according to the traditional spirit of PIME. The institute had originally gone to America in order to look for financial help. But it soon launched — thanks to the work and genius of Frs. Guido Margutti, Nicholas Maestrini, Casto Marrapese, and others — into a vast promotional campaign to make PIME known, find friends and benefactors, build seminaries, etc. The two different visions — promotion and fund-raising on one side and seminary formation on the other (especially with the grave problems which emerged in the field of theology after Vatican II) — were often in conflict.

The regional superior from 1972–1976, Fr. Charles Minck, who came out of Maryglade Seminary, tried to reduce the influx of promotion and external activities of

PIME in America. His line of thought in those years was constantly in conflict with that of Fr. Maestrini, who then went to Florida to found a retirement home for aging PIME members in Tequesta and continue with work of promoting mission.[11] It was a difficult period for PIME in America, which Fr. Maestrini remembers as extremely negative.[12]

Here's what Fr. Luigi Maggioni recalls:

> Fr. Minck was a great worker, very intelligent, austere, and — as far I'm concerned — a saint. He had a philosophy which was different than Maestrini's and it would take too long to recount all of the contrasts of that period. Minck was a child of his times, 1968, and of all the ideas there were in that period on the poverty of the church. The rich, he said, had to help because it was their duty. So he didn't care too much for the initiatives like Golf Day, and he abolished them for several years.
>
> Fr. Maestrini had put together the board with laymen to manage Maryglade, which he presented as a work of prestige for PIME for having friends and finances. Fr. Minck wanted the seminary to be directed only by the fathers. Maestrini

---

[11]Even today, at the age of 89, Fr. Maestrini is active in promotion. With the help of Fr. Pasquale Persico, with whom he lives, he raises a significant amount of funds to aid the missions and publishes a newsletter and books to make the institute known.

[12] I myself, speaking with some lay friends of PIME in Detroit, heard the position held by Fr. Minck judged negatively, at least in the field of missionary promotion. One member of PIME's Golf Day Committee told me, "We no longer knew if PIME wanted us or not, if we were helpful to the missionaries or not, and if we should continue helping them or not..."

thought big and didn't worry about going into debt because he knew that the debts would eventually be paid off, as is American logic. Minck, on the other hand, looked at the little things, and was always trying to reduce and cut back. Basically, they just weren't made to understand each other.

Fr. Carlo Brivio, who was vice regional superior with Fr. Minck, adds,

Fr. Minck lived a very austere lifestyle. He slept with the radiators off and without a pillow, he ate very little and maintained simplicity in everything — a little De Foucald. He was a mystic, of German background, not American; his feet didn't touch the earth. He had no use for Maestrini's methods which were always aimed towards promotion. Maestrini used the seminaries as instruments of promotion; he always presented the students in meetings and celebrations to show that we deserved to be helped. Minck, on the other hand, was more focused on the seminary in itself and the formation it had to offer. I didn't agree with Minck about a lot of things, but I understood his basic tendencies.

You also need to remember that we PIME members were seen too much in the American church and in the Diocese of Detroit with all of those initiatives that the newspapers, radio, and television were always talking about. Maestrini had managed to make many important friends and carry out projects that American priests hadn't

been able to, Some disagreement and maybe
even jealousy was inevitable, all the more so
since they were fund-raising initiatives, even
though they were for the missions.

CHAPTER IV

THE MISSIONARY IDEAL IN THE MASS MEDIA

IT IS NOT POSSIBLE TO UNDERSTAND PIME IN NORTH AMERICA, nor anywhere else in the world for that matter, if we do not continually return to the nature of the institute, as described in article one of its constitution:

> Within the church, which is the universal sacrament of salvation, the Pontifical Institute for Foreign Missions recognizes as its own purpose the conducting of missionary activity and, in particular, the evangelization of peoples and groups of people who are not yet Christian. Out of all the vast range of missionary activities described in *"Ad Gentes"*, P.I.M.E. chooses and designates as its priority the commitment to announce the gospel to non-Christians. It shall give this task first priority in the assignment of personnel and funds, and in the search for new fields of work and methods of work.

When speaking of PIME in North America, this priority and charism need to be kept in mind. It is a gift of the Spirit which we must communicate to the entire church, and in particular to the local churches in which we are present. This is the basis for the promotional work that PIME carries out in America; that is, spreading enthusiasm for the missionary ideal among the baptized.

The missionary ideal is a gift from PIME to America

As we know from chapter I, PIME first came to the United States in order to look for economic help for the missions and the institute, which had been devastated during World War II. But how does one find help? By mission education, making the missions and missionaries known and loved, proposing the missionary vocation as an ideal to young people, requesting prayers for the missions and aid for the projects and necessitates which are particularly worthy of being helped.

The missionary ideal — the foundational characteristic of PIME — is a gift which we offer to North America, a contribution to the profound evangelization of the American people. There is no Christian life if there is no missionary spirit, as the encyclical *Redemptoris Missio* (#2) insists:

> For in the church's history, missionary drive has always been a sign of vitality, just as its lessening is a sign of a crisis of faith... For missionary activity renews the church, revitalizes faith and Christian identity, and offers fresh enthusiasm and new incentive. Faith is strengthened when it is given to others! It is in commitment to the church's universal mission that the new evangelization of Christian peoples will find inspiration and support.

During PIME's first years in North America, when we were still unknown, missionary promotion and fund-raising were carried out on a personal level by the individual missionaries through their priestly ministry, parish mission appeals, friendships, and personal activities. The Lord blessed PIME's beginnings in the States and there are many signs which prove it. One example is the construction of the seminary in Newark, Ohio in 1955–1956, made possible by a donation from Mr. Augustine P. Wehrle, a friend of Bishop Michael J. Ready of Columbus.

It's a story worth being told in order to demonstrate the difficulties which were overcome thanks to the great generosity of God's people. Mr. Wehrle (76 years old in 1953) had never married and had accumulated, in a lifetime of work, considerable economic means. He was looking for a worthy charitable cause, and the bishop of Columbus told him about PIME. Mr. Wehrle proposed donating a large agricultural property (more than 500 acres) on which to build a seminary, as well as a sizable contribution of cash for the construction.

The bishop of Columbus jumps over PIME's gate

Frs. Maestrini and Rossi, who had visited Mr. Wehrle with the bishop, were touched by this generous gesture and gladly accepted the gift. But a short time later, Mr. Wehrle told the bishop that he was convinced that PIME had neither the experience nor the will to manage the farm and build the seminary. For this reason, he decided to donate the land and money to another religious institute. Afterwards, he repeated his refusal to Maestrini and to the vicar general of PIME, Fr. Augusto Lombardi, who was then visiting the States (spring 1954).

In the meantime, PIME's high school and college students were becoming more numerous; there was a great need for a seminary, so they began looking for other properties which were for sale. Just a year later, in March 1955, Mr. Wehrle wrote to Maestrini sending him 2,000 dollars and thanking him for his Christmas card. But he complained that PIME had given him no sufficient guarantees that they would be able to make appropriate use of his proposed donation.

Maestrini went with Fr. Antimo Boerio on March 15 to see Mr. Wehrle, who asked to see PIME's accounts in order to know if the institute was able to build a seminary or not. Maestrini responded immediately with a counter-proposal: within three months, PIME would present the architectural and financial plans for the construction of the seminary, the personnel to manage the farm, and 150,000 dollars in the bank destined for the construction of the seminary. As his end of the bargain, Wehrle would donate his property to PIME and 150,000 dollars in cash to match those raised by the institute for the seminary.

Mr. Wehrle accepted the challenge and confided to Maestrini that he had been in contact with the Trappists in order to donate his property to them. But they wanted more than the 500 acres he was offering, and Wehrle would have had to buy another nearby property to unite it to his and then give it to the Trappists. Thus, he once again had decided to make his offer to PIME!

Maestrini had the plans for the seminary drawn up, obtained a letter of credit for 150,000 dollars (based upon the worth of PIME's properties) from the Belgian-American Bank, and named Brother John Pillonetto, an agricultural expert, as supervisor of the farm which had to be carried on by the same farmers who worked for Wehrle. But this time the obstacle came from the superior general, Fr. Luigi Risso, who scolded Maestrini for trying to bite off more than he could chew. Fr. Risso didn't approve of the "American dynamism" that was animating PIME in the States. But then, after a fiery exchange of letters, he gave permission to accept Mr. Wehrle's donation. In July 1955, Wehrle examined and approved the documentation offered by Maestrini and signed the act of donation for the property and cash.

But not everything was settled. Maestrini went to tell Bishop Ready that he had obtained the donation from Wehrle after much effort and pain. The bishop was a bit put off, even infuriated; nobody had advised him that PIME had again made contacts with Wehrle and that the affair had so easily been concluded. He knew only that the Trappists had refused, so he had started looking for another religious institute which might accept the generous gift and he had already found one interested in the proposal.

Maestrini humbly begged his forgiveness, and wrote a long letter explaining step by step the entire process and showing that he had absolutely no desire of cutting the bishop out of it. He then added that, should the bishop and Mr. Wehrle find another institute which could give better guarantees than PIME for a seminary, he would be ready to give the property back. This sincerity unsettled Bishop Ready, who was angry but also very close to PIME and grateful for the work which Frs. Sala and Marrapese were doing in his diocese. He telephoned Maestrini and cordially told him that everything was settled: "You didn't advise me because you forgot; now let's just put it behind us."

Bishop Ready's affection for PIME had not diminished. Fr. John Boracco, who was rector in Newark during the construction of the seminary (1955–1956), remembers,

> Bishop Ready really loved PIME. He helped us every time we went to visit him; if a missionary was visiting our seminary, we al-

ways took him to the bishop and the bishop helped him. He came often to visit with us and followed the construction with great interest.

One time on a Sunday afternoon, I went to see how the construction was going and I found Bishop Ready there with his secretary. We weren't yet living there — we were in Columbus — and the entire area was closed off. I asked him, "How did you manage to get in with the gate locked?." The bishop answered me, "We jumped it. Why? Is it prohibited?" "No," I responded, "It's just that I've never seen a bishop jump over a locked gate before."

When we called him to bless and inaugurate the seminary in Newark, he gave such a moving speech, saying among other things, "This is the missionary seminary of our diocese, the missionary seminary of Columbus."

John Travolta dances for the missions

Another interesting story which is worth telling deals with Fr. Casto Marrapese, whose ability to make and maintain friendships is in no way inferior to that of Fr. Maestrini. The founding of the seminary in Oakland, New Jersey was due to his efforts.

PIME in America, founded in Detroit thanks to Margutti's friendship with Cardinal Mooney, had from the very beginning planned a residence and a seminary on the east coast, given that around half of all American Catholics are concentrated with-

74

in a range of 200 miles from New York. The opportunity presented itself in 1951. On February 18, 1951, Pope Pius XII beatified Fr. Alberic Crescitelli, a PIME priest martyred in China in 1900. Two brothers, who were his nephews, lived near New York and contacted PIME. Ulisse De Stefano, son of one of Blessed Alberic's sisters, stated that he was ready to donate a plot of land in Emerson, New Jersey, to PIME in order to build a seminary.

Thus, Fr. Marrapese left Columbus in 1952 and was sent to New Jersey in order to establish a PIME presence there. Here is his story:

I went to live in a parish in Emerson, waiting for Ulisse De Stefano to donate the promised land. For four years I served the parish in every way and I did some missionary promotion. I did various things (preached mission appeals, showed missionary films in the schools, held meetings and bingo parties with friends, visited the families, helped spread missionary newspapers, etc.) and I made friends and gathered funds for the missions and for PIME. After four years, even having helped the missions quite a bit, I had 75,000 dollars in the bank which was earmarked for construction of the seminary. But still the land promised by De Stefano didn't come. So I bought a little house near that property and named it the Blessed Alberic Mission House. Then, continuing to serve the parish in Emerson and other nearby parishes even though it meant great sacrifice, I began to promote mission in a big way.

One day I met the Italian wife of a film director from Twentieth Century Fox, the largest movie studio of the time. I became a friend of the family, and the husband allowed me free use of a huge theater for one or two evenings each year. We would show films before they were released to the general public, and the profit would be donated to PIME and its missions. We also put on some live shows, in which there were songs, dances, and plays of a religious or missionary theme. We filled the theater because I had obtained, always through friends, the free collaboration of performers, scenery makers, sound technicians, dancers, singers, etc.

In that field, when you know one, you know them all; and to a missionary who asks a favor nobody says no. The very famous John Travolta danced on that stage for PIME's missions, two years in a row. He was already very good but I suppose you could say that our presentations are what launched his career. Even the task of selling tickets was an adventure. There was a committee of lay people who worked so hard for months — they and their wives and children, their relatives and friends, etc. If Americans adopt an idea or a project, they know how to be so generous. The Lord helped us and we always filled that theater, especially since that director from Twentieth Century Fox had told me, "I'll continue giving you the theater only if you can fill it; I can't afford the bad publicity of having it half empty."

The birth of the seminary in Oakland, New Jersey

"Naturally I was always on the go," continues Fr. Marrapese.

> Between trips, visits, telephone calls, letters, lunches and suppers, I never had a free moment. I kept a diary in those years, and day by day I wrote down all the places I went, the people I met or visited, the telephone calls that I received or made, and the letters which I wrote. Now, paging through the yellowed pages of these notebooks, I often ask myself how I did it? Especially with those distances?
>
> Then Fr. Biagio Simonetti came in 1955, and he helped me out a lot[1] I remained in New Jersey until 1967 and I built the seminary in Oakland.

In 1958, after years of hopes and delusions, it was quite clear that Ulisse De Stefano wasn't going to give the promised property to PIME. The archbishop of Newark, Bishop Thomas A. Boland, admired the work which the PIME missionaries were doing in his diocese, so he helped the institute find another possibility in Oakland, some 40 minutes from downtown Manhattan. The owner, John Fiorilla, ceded the land (20 acres) in 1959 for a special price: 125,000 dollars. Later Marrapese bought another 13 acres of wooded land for 25,000 dol-

---

[1] In 1959, Fr. Biagio Simonetti departed for Brazil where he founded a city, Freiburgo, in the state of Santa Catarina. See Piero Gheddo's volume, *Missione Brasile, I cinquant'anni del PIME nel Brasile del Sud e in Mato Grosso*, EMI, Bologna 1996, pages 148–151.

lars and paid for it all with what he had gathered during the previous years precisely for this purpose.

The seminary opened its doors to 11 high-school students in September, 1961, using the already existing house of the previous owner. In the following years, Fr. Marrapese and his collaborators built the new seminary (costing 40,000 dollars), which Archbishop Boland inaugurated on August 19, 1965. It stayed open as a seminary until the middle of the 1970s. PIME's roots in America's East Coast were still not mature. So when the vocation crisis grew to alarming proportions in America (as in Italy and all of the Christian West) in the years following Vatican Council II (1962–1965), keeping a seminary open in that part of the States was impossible. The seminary in Newark, Ohio, on the other hand, remained open until 1990.

The failed attempt at a Catholic "Life"

Between 1952 and 1960, PIME in America established its missionary promotion programs, which continue even today (as we'll see in chapter VII).

The first important step was the founding of the monthly magazine *Catholic Life Around the World* in January 1954, as a replacement for the *St. Peter and Paul Bulletin* (begun in 1952). Fr. Maestrini's idea, which was recommended to him by an expert in public relations and by the director of a publicity agency, was to launch a monthly family magazine for a large audience. It didn't have to be exclusively missionary, but with general articles adapted to the American public, introducing missionary experiences and news about the church in the world and, naturally, news about PIME.

The plan was for *Catholic Life* (with the subtitle *around the World* in small letters) to be the Catholic version of the well-known magazine, *Life*, which was then circulating millions of copies! The basic principle of Maestrini's life has always been: "Think big, plan big, and aim high." Always optimistic and grandiose in his projects Maestrini didn't, however, take into account that *Life* was published by the powerful *Time* magazine. Behind *Catholic Life*, however, there was only a small foreign institute which was struggling to survive in American society.

But even before that, the principle difficulty came from the Italian missionaries who were helping Maestrini in the States. They were against the 32-page, small-format magazine which spoke so little about missions and missionaries. On May 18, 1954, in a meeting between PIME's vicar general, Fr. Augusto Lombardi, and the PIME members in America, there was a kind of uprising against the magazine. The vicar general ordered that the magazine be made 100 per cent missionary, giving them until January 1956 to change the nature of *Catholic Life.*

Today Maestrini admits,

> My plan could not have succeeded because it was not within the nature and structure of our society nor within PIME's financial capability to organize and publish a magazine of the type Mr. Frank Hall and I had envisioned. But what I want to emphasize now is that, thanks to God, I obeyed and obedience was rewarded. Under the able editorship of Bob Bayer, *Catholic Life* became a great success for PIME; we managed to arrive at around 30,000 subscriptions. The magazine has been the principle instrument for promoting the various activities which we have

undertaken to help the missions.[2]

The missionary museum and two books in English

PIME's promotion work, since the very beginning, has always had a wide purpose: not simply to cultivate the little garden of friends, benefactors, and parishes in which our missionaries were performing their ministry, but to send out news, messages, and missionary appeals to the American church and society with the most modern and most original means. In the meantime, the traditional forms of promoting mission were continued: parish mission appeals, films for the students of the Catholic schools, the formation of groups of PIME friends and the "guild ladies" for the seminaries, and summer camps for youth desiring to dedicate themselves to missionary life.

In September of 1954, Fr. Guido Margutti returned to the States in order to establish a missionary museum in PIME's headquarters in Detroit. Since the time he had returned to Italy (October 1949), Fr. Margutti had renewed and updated the institute's missionary museum in the mother house in Milan (founded shortly after PIME's foundation in 1855) with new display items from the missions. Margutti had spent his own money and that of his family. Today the PIME museum in Milan, under the watchful eye of Fr. Mario Marazzi (who was a missionary in Hong Kong), is counted among the most prestigious of public museums with thousands of visitors each year, especially school students brought there by their teachers.

Margutti returned to Detroit in 1954 and brought

---

2 See *P.I.M.E. in the United States. The First Twenty-Five Years*, op. cit., page 196.

seven crates of material from Asia, Africa, and the Brazilian Amazon. Thus was born "The Oriental Art Museum", inaugurated by Cardinal Edward Mooney on September 19, 1954, with good coverage by Detroit's newspapers.

In 1954 and 1955, PIME published two books: *Forward with Christ* by Fr. Paolo Manna, and *In God's Hand* by Elio Gasperetti. The first book is a translation and reworking of the famous *The Workers are Few* written by PIME's Superior General (1924–1934) Fr. Paolo Manna. The second book is the biography of Blessed Alberic Crescitelli, martyred in China in 1900 and beatified by Pope Pius XII on February 18, 1951.

Other works published included a monthly color mission poster put out by PIME in Italy from 1956 up to the present with the title, *Your Kingdom Come!* It consists in a monthly missionary intention from the Apostolate of Prayer, a large photograph, and statistics and quotes, the basis of prayer intentions. In the States it was published from 1958 to 1980, with a distribution of 1,500 copies. In addition, calendars, Christmas cards, and other books and brochures were produced.

The failure of a benefit performance for PIME

Beginning in the mid 1950s, PIME began to stimulate interest in mission in new and original ways. Such efforts, those of Fr. Maestrini in Detroit and Fr. Marrapese in New Jersey, had a great impact. The success of the promotion efforts permitted PIME to make itself known, to build its seminaries, and to provide great help to the missions, launching financing programs for the projects of various missionaries.

It should be added that while the promotional activities of the center in Detroit and of Fr. Marrapese raised the necessary sums for the construction of the seminaries of Newark, Maryglade, and Oakland, the maintenance of these seminaries depended almost entirely upon the ministerial activities and missionary promotion activities of the fathers who worked there as rectors, administrators, formation directors and teachers. Fr. Henry Paleari's report to the institute's general chapter in 1971 reads:

> Fr. Maestrini's office in Detroit has built but it does not provide ongoing maintenance of the region. Especially in these last ten years, the fathers working in the seminary have earned between 200,000 dollars and 250,000 dollars each year through their ministerial work, work with the guild ladies, and other activities. With this money, they maintain the seminaries and have saved a modest amount for the future.

Fr. Maestrini's first great promotional event in the field of entertainment turned out less than successful. He went to New York with a good friend, Bob DeMascio, to invite a famous Italian-American singer, Perry Como, to come and perform for the benefit of PIME. But they couldn't even get in touch with him.

The "Association of PIME Friends" insisted upon having some kind of show, so they signed a contract for 16,000 dollars with the Olympia Theater in Detroit for a show called "Super Circus". They needed to sell tickets but, notwithstanding the commitment of friends and the advertisement of the newspapers, many of the tickets remained unsold. Maestrini concludes, "The operation finished with a loss of 3,000 dollars. It was a hard but healthy lesson. Never again during my administration did we organize an event of that kind, with big organizational expenses and doubtful economic gain." In spite of the disappointment, the experience wasn't negative because PIME's name was placed in the public eye, especially in Detroit; this permitted Maestrini to approach people with other initiatives, which were, in fact, successful.

The Knights of Charity award

One event must be recalled as a demonstration of the new way of making friends for the missions: the Knights of Charity Award Dinner. There are many associations of knights in the world: of Malta, of the Holy Sepulchre, of the Templars, of Columbus, and others. The only ones missing were the Knights of Charity. They were thus invented by the Friends of PIME Association with a formula attentive to the sensibility of America. Every year a personality noted in the field of charity would be chosen and honored with the Knights of Charity Award given during a big dinner.

Every day, the mass media reports thousands of negative news items about society, which often leads to pessimism: violence, robberies, corruption, drugs, murders, divorces, abortions, etc. Each year PIME awards the title "Knight of Charity" to a person who has distinguished himself in charitable action, and who can serve as a model for others, especially the younger generation.

Today there are many such dinners and awards, recognizing works of charity, love of the poor, education, service to the church or to one's city, faithfulness to marriage, etc. PIME's Knights of Charity Dinner was one of the first and represented a model for how to honor a positive hero of American society.

The first dinner was held on September 19, 1954 at the Sheraton Cadillac Hotel in Detroit; the second on October 2, 1955; the third on October 6, 1956. Since then, this celebration of charity has been celebrated nearly every year and has honored famous and not-so-famous individuals: social workers, actors, union members, doctors, founders of charitable works, and, naturally, missionaries. One of these was Dr. Marcello Candia who received the award in 1981. The owner of several industries in Milan, in 1965 at the age of 49 he sold all of his industries and came with us PIME Missionaries to the Amazon to spend all of his money and even his very life.[3]

The award dinner has hosted between 300 and 800 people (depending on the year) from Detroit and the nearby cities. Each makes a donation to PIME for his or her participation, but also as a sign of the distinction of having been invited. Each celebration becomes a city happening which is covered by newspapers and televisions and makes PIME known. Then there is the net gain from the event which helps PIME and its missions.

Since 1959 the award has truly become ecumenical. In that year, the Maryglade board of trustees (made up of missionaries and lay persons), which organized the dinner, decided to give the award each year not just to one but to three deserving persons of varying religious traditions whether Catholic, Protestant, Jewish or Muslim. The award and the dinner have thus become a sign of cooperation and unity where racial and religious tensions exist. The aim is to hold up these heroes of charity, who dedicate themselves to the poor, to the ill, and to the marginalized as models before society at large; to overcome all barriers between people and to

---

[3] Marcello Candia, who died on August 31, 1983, is considered by many to be a saint. In 1991 Cardinal Carlo Maria Martini, Archbishop of Milan, began his cause for canonization, which has already reached the Roman phase. The postulator for the cause is Fr. Piero Gheddo.

create an event in which everyone can participate. In fact, its in this very sign of love for one's neighbor that the unity of a people and a nation can be found.

The success of the Knights of Charity Dinner was so extraordinary in American society that it caught the attention of the national media. In September 1965, *TIME* magazine published an article on fund-raisers, focusing on persons with the skill of gathering funds for beneficial works; they named Fr. Nicholas Maestrini as one of the best in the United States and published his photo. He was ranked second, after an Anglican bishop from California who raised 60,000 dollars in one evening (while Maestrini was able to raise 45,000 dollars) Remember, naturally, that we're talking about 1965 dollars! In order to evaluate this recognition, it should be noted that fund-raising is one of the most appreciated abilities in America; such recognition of a foreigner at the highest national level really means a lot.

Helping the missions by playing golf

Another ingenious initiative which PIME set up in the States is the Golf Day which has been held in June every year since 1957. In the second half of the 1950s, it was urgent to involve many people in order to find the funds necessary for the construction of the seminary in Newark.

The architect, Victor Basso, had planned a bell tower with a Chinese style roof and a cross on top, which would become characteristic of PIME in Newark. The cost was 8,000 dollars. PIME's promotional office prepared a letter asking for help and sent it to many friends in Detroit. One of these, Frank D. Stella, an emerging Detroit businessman,[4] went to Fr. Maestrini

---

[4]Even today Frank D. Stella is committed to helping PIME as a member of

with his friend, Tom Angott. They each gave him 1,000 dollars saying, "We want to help the missionaries in another way, too. Let's organize a golf outing to raise money for PIME."

The idea of playing golf and raising money for the missions in this way had never crossed the minds of Fr. Maestrini nor the other missionaries. The proposal appeared to them, at first, as something a bit farfetched, unattainable. Rather, after consulting the association of PIME friends, they found people who were understanding and willing to collaborate.

Thus began the preparations for the first Golf Day, in June 1957 with 200 participants. The following year 300 participated, and Golf Day has grown to the point that in 1997, 1200 tickets were sold. The outing is celebrated on the second Tuesday of June, and the organization begins in March with a special committee. They need to prepare the day's program, the prizes for the drawing, the ticket sales, publicity, course arrangements, etc.

But Golf Day isn't the only event which is organized in order to help the institute and the missions. Each PIME residence has created meetings with friends and various initiatives. In Newark, Ohio the annual Labor Day ox roast draws about 3,000 persons per year; there is a smaller version of the Golf Day in Newark as well. The seminary in Oakland, New Jersey, sold in 1995, continued holding two large flea markets, one in June and one in September, right up to the end. These initiatives, organized and carried out primarily by the PIME

---

the Lay Advisory Board. He is one of the most active businessmen in Detroit, and also a great patron of the arts and music. For example, he spearheaded the renovation of Michigan Opera Theater (MOT) and Orchestra Hall in Detroit. The director of MOT has described him as "a modern Renaissance man."

Guilds in each location, are not only meant to raise money for PIME and its missions, but also to make PIME known in an enjoyable way.

"I have a wife and three children; I can't live with the lepers"

The basic concept behind the mission promotion Maestrini carried on in the States is one which he had in China while announcing the message of Jesus to the non-Christians: don't dwell upon small individual actions, but launch messages to the largest amount of people possible, sowing seeds of goodness which, with the help of God, can bring forth fruit among friends.

This is the reason why PIME's promotion work in America has put a lot of emphasis upon the printed word, events designed to attract large numbers of people, the involvement of lay friends and public relations experts, mass mailings of letters and brochures to raise interest in the missions, and finally the production of films.

In 1953, Maestrini went to California where he visited different film studios and inquired about the prices. He found that a half hour professionally brought filming costs to around 60,000 dollars. That was a prohibitive sum for PIME in those days! Maestrini showed a short film sent to him by our missionaries in Hong Kong and received a completely negative judgment on it. Then he met the young director William F. Deneen, to whom Maestrini proposed a plan for five documentaries which were to be filmed in PIME's Asian missions of those days: Japan, Hong Kong, Burma, India, and Bangladesh. Deneen committed himself to making the five films for 100,000 dollars since he was going to be in the Asia for other work.

Bill was enthusiastic about working with the missionaries, but when he heard that he would have to film a documentary in a leprosarium in Burma, he replied, "I have a wife and three children; I can't live with lepers. I'll have to think about it." Then he put his trust in God's goodness. In a period of four months, he visited PIME's missions and brought home precious material from which to make four documentaries which were, in the States and in Italy, the only PIME missionary films for at least 20–25 years. They were of a beauty, simplicity, and force which have yet to be equaled.

The most famous was *The Touch of His Hand*. It narrates the story of a girl who discovers she has leprosy just on the night before her wedding, and of Fr. Cesare Colombo — doctor and director of the Leprosy Center in Kengtung, Burma — who heals her. The film is touching for its plot and the naturalness of the actors, and is grandiose for the nature scenes and the participation of large numbers of Burmese in the dances. In 1959 the film won first prize in Belgium in the International Festival of missionary films.

Deneen made two other trips for PIME: one to Kengtung, Burma in order to continue the story of the Leprosy Center of Kengtung *(The Happy City)* and the other to the Amazon in 1963 to produce *Latitude Zero*.

Helping the missions a priority

The aid sent to the missions is the most important aspect of missionary promotion in the United States, and certainly the most significant for PIME. The various promotional activities are oriented at making the missions and missionaries known and loved, and obtaining for them prayers and economic help, as well as vocations. The requests are precisely worded, guaranteeing their serious nature and their going directly to help the missionaries. In recent years, regional superior Fr.

Bruno Piccolo says, PIME in North America has been sending between one million and 1.5 million dollars to the missions each year. Here are the major services done for the missions:

1. Native Seminarians Project in the dioceses founded by PIME. The youth to be adopted are selected by the rectors of the seminaries, who send their photos and personal stories. In America are families who commit themselves to giving a small monthly sum, sufficient for the maintenance of a student in the seminary.

Other forms of collaborating with evangelization in the missions include the construction of chapels and help for the formation of catechists.

2. The Foster Parents Mission Club began in 1958 with a request from the bishop of Kengtung (Burma), Bishop Ferdinando Guercilena. Joyce Daigue (now Dr. Joyce Petrak) came up with the idea to help Bishop Guercilena by asking families in the U.S. and Canada to "adopt" disadvantaged children in his missions. This program has developed into the most successful form of help in North America. In 1961 PIME already had a thousand adoptive parents for children in Burma, Bangladesh, and India. The recruiting of new members is entrusted to the individual "foster parents", who commit themselves to making the association known, to publishing articles and advertisements in local newspapers, and to creating little groups of family and friends who collaborate for this reason.

In 1973 there were 2,700 participants (adopting around 3,300 children). Since then, the numbers have held rather steady: 4,500 to 5,000 children adopted by 3,000 to 3,500 sponsors from the U.S., Canada, Germany, Hong Kong, Belgium, Spain and Malaysia. The present director of the program, Alice Marino, prepares a quarterly newsletter to keep the benefactors in touch with the happenings at the missions where their adopted children are located.

3. The Leprosy Relief Society. This activity for lepers began with William Deneen's aforementioned film, *The Touch of His Hand*, and from two visits to Detroit in the 1950s; one by the bishop of Kengtung, Bishop Ferdinando Guercilena, and the other by Fr. Cesare Colombo, the director of the leprosy center in Kengtung. The program was then widened to include other leprosy centers in Bangladesh, India, Africa, and the Brazilian Amazon.

4. Other forms of helping the missions are focused upon specific requests or projects. For example, sewing machines are provided for girls' training centers; aid is given in cases of natural disasters such as earthquakes in India and floods in Bangladesh; books, medicines, agricultural supplies and so on are sent in response to specific requests of missionaries and bishops.

To conclude, here's a reflection by Fr. Nicholas Maestrini: "The search for funding for the missions is a laborious, complicated, long, difficult, and above all delicate undertaking. It requires a great amount of tact, humility and especially patience and research on the part of the personnel of the public relations office."[5]

Fr. Maestrini goes on to describe the work which he and his collaborators carry out and the difficulties they encounter. Not only are there difficulties with regards to the benefactors, but the missionaries themselves create problems because of imprecise requests, not saying thank you, or not sending documentation on how they've spent the sums received, etc. There's also the challenge of following up on each person and making

---

[5] "The American region on behalf of the missionaries in the field — The difficult job of searching", in *Il Vincolo*, January-March 1967, 17–18.

PIME Seminary — Newark, Ohio
The seminary was closed in 1991. Today it
functions as a mission retreat center.

Boys attending PIME summer camp
at Newark, Ohio.

The late Bishop Michael J. Ready
blessing the cornerstone of the
PIME seminary in Newark, Ohio.

Maryglade Seminary, Memphis, Michigan
Closed in 1972 and eventually sold.

Left to right:
Fr. John Boracco,
Fr. Nicholas Maestrini,
Fr. Dominic Rossi, the
Architect, and
Fr. Silvio Colosio,
poring over plans for
Maryglade Seminary,
which was opened
September 10, 1960

Fr. Carlo Brivio
with retreatants
in Maryglade
museum — 1967

Regional Headquarters and Mission Office
Detroit, Michigan

Fr. Sandy Garzarelli was the first PIME priest ordained, 1960. He left PIME for the Archdiocese of Philadelphia in 1970.

In 1995 Fr. Sandy Garzarelli rejoined PIME as an associate priest. Above Frs. Steve Baumbusch and Bruno Piccolo see him off for Papua New Guinea — 1997.

Top: Our Lady Queen of Missions Seminary in Oakland, New Jersey. Now closed.

Middle: Promotion Center, Clinton Township (Fraser), Michigan. Now a Carmelite Monastery.

Right: Robert Bayer, Editor of *Catholic Life* and Public Relations Director, 1962–1990.

Roy, New
Mexico
Mission

Fr. Dominic
Rossi before
Old San
Francesco
Church,
Detroit

Brother Pius in
print shop in the
early days.

Men in Charge in North America

Fr. Guido Margutti (1947–1949)

Fr. Dante Magri (1949–1951)

Fr. Henry Paleari
(Regional Superior 1969–1973)

Fr. Charles Minck
(Regional Superior 1973–1977)

Fr. Luigi Maggioni
(Regional Superior 1977–1989)

(left) Fr. Bruno Piccolo (1995–   )
(right) Fr. Steve Baumbusch
(1989–1995) Regional Superiors

Fr. Nicholas Maestrini was Regional Superior from 1951–1969. Photos are of him in 1991 and (insert) as a young missioner.

Knights of Charity Award Dinner 1969

Mr. Perry Como, Mr. Frank Stella, Fr. Maestrini, Knights of Charity Award Dinner 1984

Fr. Bruno Venturin, PIME, Msgr. Leo DeBarry and Fr. Dominic Rossi, PIME. Msgr. DeBarry directed the Society for the Propagation of Faith in Detroit in PIME's early days in the U.S.

Cardinal Edward Mooney.
Detroit Archbishop, 1937–1958

Above: Mission Center in Cuanacaxtitlán, Guerrero, Mexico.

Left: Fr. Steve Baumbusch, who opened the mission in Mexico in 1992, serves communion to the Mixtec parishioners.

Fr. Luigi Maggioni (center) with a Franciscan Sister of St. Joseph and a PIME seminarian.

PIME Retirement House and Mission Center — Tequesta, Florida

Fr. Nicholas Maestrini in Tequesta with visitor Fr. Pasquale Persico, who resides in Tequesta.

Fr. Nicholas Ruggiero (left) and Fr. Bruno Piccolo at Blessed Agnes Tsao Kouying Mission near Toronto, Canada

PIME priests gathered with Cardinal Adam Maida of Detroit for centennial celebration of San Francesco Church, October 1996.

In order to familiarize himself with a PIME mission Seminarian Guy Snyder (left) travels in Japan with Fr. Francis Mossholder.

Fr. Claudio Corti with little Mixtec friends in the mission of Cuanacaxtitlán, Guerrero, Mexico.

Gathered together in assembly (1995) were most of the priests and the one brother of the U.S./Canada Region. Top, left to right: Fathers Raphael Magni, Claudio Corti, George Paleari, T. Warren Sattler, Dino Vanin, Giulio Schiavi, Luigi Acerbi. Front row, left to right: Fathers Nicholas Maestrini, John Boracco, Pasquale Persico, Ronnie Boccali, visitor Gianpiero Bruni, Bruno Piccolo, Steve Baumbusch, Nicholas Ruggiero, Angelo Villa, Luigi Maggioni, Brother Tony Testori, Fathers Edward Miley and Casto Marrapese. Missing were Fathers James Coleman, Luciano Ghezzi, Dominic Rossi and Carlo Sala.

1996 Mission Office staff, Detroit. Back row, left to right: Virginia Szczepanski, Robert Rawlings, Louise Wright, Margaret Fleming, Barbara Rubaie, Paul Witte, Fr. Bruno Piccolo. Middle row: Eva Gornowicz, Judith Lentine, Donald Kuester, Maria Biernacki, Fr. John Boracco, Fr. Angelo Villa, Betty Burski, Edward Burski. Seated: Alice Marino, Sr. Aida, Sr. Rubi, Sr. Magdalena (Franciscan Sisters of St. Joseph)

friends with the benefactors:

> ...visiting them when they're ill, being present at their funerals of family members, and accepting invitations to their marriages and luncheon parties even if it means ruining your stomach or losing hours and hours of sleep. Everything is always done for the love of God and our missionary commitment towards the people.

CHAPTER V

THE WORK OF PIME IN AMERI-
CAN PARISHES

IN MY LIFE AS A PRIEST, I'VE NEVER EXPERIENCED the priesthood like here in Detroit, in the parish of the Italians. In the missions, in Bangladesh and in Papua New Guinea, I was very busy on the social and educational levels, but in terms of pastoral work and evangelization, I'm even busier here. In Detroit I do real missionary work, in the sense that I must often start from zero: I meet quite a few "baptized pagans" (and some not even baptized), without any knowledge of Christianity.

These are the words of Father Giulio Schiavi, who has been the pastor since January 1, 1997 of San Francesco Parish in Mount Clemens near Detroit. He is most enthusiastic about this pastoral ministry.

The bell tower of San Francesco Church in the Amazon

San Francesco in Detroit was the first parish entrusted to PIME in the States (January 11, 1949) and the only one that we still operate today. San Francesco was started in 1896, and the first pastor, Father Francis Beccherini, a Scalabrinian, remained there for 48 years, bringing it to great heights of glory and efficiency. In 1944 he was replaced by Father Emilio Capano, who rebuilt the church, which had been almost completely destroyed by fire. On January 11, 1949, Capano was transferred to a larger parish and Father Guido Margutti was named parochial vicar. The parish was entrusted to PIME.

At the time of the foundation of San Francesco on Brewster Street, the district was mostly inhabited by Italian families, who formed a "Little Italy." Then, as they improved their economic conditions, many went to live in areas outside the city, quite distant from the church. The neighborhood came to be inhabited by African Americans. The last Italians left and the parish school was closed. On Sundays the church was attended only by the elderly of a few Italian families. In 1949 the missionaries of PIME began to visit the Italian families, house by house, comforting the sick, reconciling marriages, and making friends with the various regional groups (Piedmontese, Lombardi, Sicilians, Neapolitans). They succeeded to bring hundreds of families back to the church.

The pastors of San Francesco were Fr. Margutti, Fr. Dante Magri, Fr. Mario Dall'Agnol, Fr. Hector Bellinato, all former missionaries in India; Fr. Ugo Sordo (China), Fr. Giulio Cancelli (India), and Fr. Dominic Rossi, (Ethiopia and the Brazilian Amazon). The latter became pastor in 1959 and remained there for 37 years, up to December of 1996. Fr. Rossi comments:

> When I became pastor, with the help of Father Marzorati, I began to repair the church. However Cardinal Mooney told us: "Don't spend money, because this church must be torn down; I will give you a better one." We worked hard and I hoped to keep that church open. I was amazed when, a

little before Christmas of 1966, a representative of the Detroit chancery came to tell us that the church would have to be abandoned before Christmas. I managed to hold out until Christmas, but then we had to leave.

When the old church of San Francesco had to be torn down, the Italians organized protests, picketing with placards in groups of five in front of the chancery, in order to stay within the law. But there was nothing to do. The very morning after we PIME members left, the wrecking crew arrived to destroy everything, for fear that the Italians might disrupt the work. I was able to save the bell of San Francesco, and we sent it to the Amazon, where today it still calls the faithful from the bell tower of the church of San Francis in Macapà.

In Mount Clemens a Baptist church becomes Catholic

The journey of San Francesco Parish continued: first in the church of the Patronage of Saint Joseph on Gratiot Avenue (January 1, 1967), then in the church of the new PIME headquarters on Oakland Boulevard (November 15, 1969). In 1975, when PIME transferred from Oakland Boulevard to Quincy Avenue, Fr. Rossi and the people of the parish were able to purchase a small Protestant church in Mount Clemens, near Detroit.

Fr. Rossi says,

It was a Baptist church that had closed and relocated, but we didn't have the necessary money. The cardinal gave the parish

94

a loan which we repaid. Collecting funds from our parishioners we enlarged the church by about 30 feet, changed the roof and the windows, put acoustic tile everywhere, rebuilt the foundation wall of the church because it was crumbling, changed the bricks of the façade, and built the rectory and the bell tower (which alone cost 50,000 dollars). A few years ago, I purchased some nearby property to enlarge the parking lot. The centenary of the church, 1996, was celebrated with a huge get-together, with 1,200 persons gathered for the dinner. Before the meal, we celebrated Mass, and Archbishop Cardinal Adam Maida presided. He thanked the Italians and PIME for having established this parish.

I asked Fr. Rossi how many Italians are in the new San Francesco. He responded:

A difficult question. As far as registered families, there are about 350–400, certainly more than that participate in the parish. The parish is non-territorial, a personal parish for the Italians. We celebrate Mass in Italian each Sunday at 10:00 a.m. But others with a variety of ethnic backgrounds who live near the church also come: French, Polish, English, some African Americans and Vietnamese. The Italians make up about half the congregation, and some come an hour or hour and half by car for Sunday Mass.

The religious life in America contains many surprises for an Italian. For example, an average of 45–50 percent of American Catholics attend Sunday Mass (in Italy the national average is 28–30 percent; in other European countries, France and Germany for example, the frequency is 15 percent). In the States there are the territorial parishes as in Italy, but also the "national" parishes: Italian, Chinese, Mexican, Vietnamese, German, Polish, etc., in which the Mass and sermon are said in that language. The parish also becomes a meeting and socializing place for members of a given ethnic community.

On December 2, 1996 the archbishop of Detroit, Cardinal Adam Maida, raised the church of San Francesco from a mission to parish status, and on January 1,1997 Fr. Dominic Rossi was succeeded by the new pastor, Father Giulio Schiavi, who is assisted by Fr. Raffaele Magni (former missionary in the Brazilian Amazon).

"It gives me great satisfaction to work with the Italians"

Like San Francesco, the parish of St. John the Baptist in Columbus (Ohio) was also born in 1896. Entrusted to PIME on August 5, 1949 (see chapter I), its first PIME pastor was Father Charles Sala (former missionary in Ethiopia), with Father Casto Marrapese as assistant. Father Sala (1949–55) was followed as pastor by Fr. Antimo Boerio (missionary in China, 1955–1957), Fr. Ovidio Calzini (from Hong Kong, 1957–1959), Fr. Ettore Bellinato (India, 1959–1974) and finally Fr. Marrapese, who remained up to 1991. Before becoming pastor in Columbus, he had helped PIME become established in New Jersey (see chapter II).

The Italian community, saved from the danger of having to close the parish, welcomed the Italian missionaries; but, as Father Sala relates:

> We found a very difficult situation. Every-
> thing was neglected and abandoned: mice
> overran the house, eating any food that
> was left on the table or in the kitchen, even
> the soap in the sink. Fr. Petrarca had been
> a great priest, but in the last years he had
> let things go badly. Even the church was in
> a state of pitiable disrepair. The bishop was
> ready to close the parish, because no priest
> was willing to go there and put it back in
> order.

Father Sala and the other pastors of PIME after him
refurbished the church, enlarged the rectory and reor-
ganized the parish, reviving the various associations
and achieving a good Sunday attendance on the part of
the Italians. The Italian community, which flourished in
the time of Fr. Petrarca and then lapsed because of the
threat of closing the parish, was reestablished.

Today Fr. Charles says:

> The most beautiful time of my life in Ameri-
> ca were those years when I was pastor of St.
> John the Baptist in Columbus. There was
> satisfaction in working with the Italian-
> Americans. It was enough to be available for
> their needs, and they collaborated in every-
> thing with enthusiasm and generosity.

Father Sala then worked fifteen years in the semi-
nary of Newark, Ohio, and was named pastor at St.
Leonard in Heath, Ohio, another parish in the diocese of
Columbus.

Also Father Hector Bellinato has given much to the
parish of St. John the Baptist (1969–1974). Of sweet

and affectionate character, he was especially attentive to the families of the parish and to visiting the sick. He will also be remembered for the magnificent pipe organ, built on location at St. John by a famous Italian firm.

The Italian Festival in Columbus (Ohio)

After Fr. Rocco Petrarca (1913–1947), the pastor who worked the longest at St. John the Baptist, comes Fr. Casto Marrapese (1974–1991), who brought the parish to a high level of pastoral, social and cultural activity, focusing the attention of the entire city on the Italian community with many successful initiatives. His Sunday sermons, of sound doctrine and rooted in the life of the people, are gathered in the volume "Water from the Old Fountain," which has been circulated throughout and beyond the parish.[1]

Father Marrapese accomplished many works: he renovated the church and the parish hall, remodeled the rectory, etc. The first work he did, he did in memory of Fr. Petrarca, a great pastor still remembered to this day. In 1975, Fr. Marrapese dedicated a marble bust of Fr. Petrarca in front of the church. Fr. Antimo Boerio writes the following:

> The unveiling of the bust was a local event, covered by radio and television. The name of Father Petrarca was on the lips of all the Italians of Columbus and his image, via television, entered the homes of those he perhaps baptized or joined in matrimony.[2]

---

[1] An interesting book on the 100 years of the parish of St. John the Baptist in Columbus: *A Century of Faith, 1896–1996—Biography of an Italian National Parish* by Fr. Casto Marrapese, PIME, 1997; 116 pages, can be obtained from Fr. Marrapese at the PIME Mission Center, 2734 Seminary Rd., S.E., Newark, Ohio 43056-9339.

[2] Boerio A., *Memories*, PIME: Rome, 1995, 176 pages.

Fr. Marrapese adds:

> With the bust of Fr. Petrarca I gained the good will of the people and I then went forward with various projects, all with the concrete support of the parishioners. The first was to enlarge the church property, which was squeezed in among many large buildings. I purchased six small lots and created a large parking area, without which the parish would have been abandoned. Then I learned that the Dominican nuns nearby were planning to leave, so we bought some land available from them.
>
> I helped hold the Italian community together so they would attend church, because the Catholic faith is part of our most ancient tradition. I built the Italian Cultural Center, where we began to teach, have lectures, shows, dances, and concerts, We had a library and gathered together groups from different Italian regions, with their distinctive banners, folklore, food, etc.
>
> In 1980, with the collaboration of many persons, we began the Italian Festival, not on the church grounds where the traditional annual bazaar was being held, but rather on the State fairgrounds of Columbus, in a hall of 160,000 square feet, where we could have shows, dances, political meetings and sporting events. We inaugurated our festival with the three F's as our motto: "Faith, Family, Friends," and it included something for everyone: food (there were dozens of stands run by individuals or Italian restaurants), wine, art, music, liter-

ature, Italian shops, Italian books, sports, tourism in Italy and so on.

The festival has become huge and is devoted entirely to Italian things. Each year, besides the general exposition, a particular aspect of Italian life is showcased in the center of the large hall: architecture, automobiles, fashion, films. During the year I copied famous Italian paintings; they were not too bad. I exhibited them and even sold some. As could be easily understood, this Italian Festival mobilized the whole Italian community, including the Italian embassy in Washington, and growing numbers of Americans have been coming each year, some from quite far away. It was a success especially with the young people of the Italian families, in which we have restored the pride in being American of Italian descent.

Another initiative born from the Italian Festival is the scholarship for young Italians: we don't give it to those who get the most votes, but to those most in need, whose family is struggling to pay for college or university tuition.

Today the parish of St. John the Baptist, which would have been closed years ago without the PIME fathers, is now led by Fr. Mario Serraglio, an ex-member of PIME incardinated in the diocese of Columbus. What we have done there remains as a sign of our devotion to the diocese.

A second parish entrusted to PIME in the diocese of Columbus was that of St. Leonard in Heath, from 1970 to 1981. The pastor, Fr. Charles Sala, found a difficult situation because this parish too had been neglected and was in danger of closing. Fr. Charles says:

> When I became pastor in 1970, there was a debt of 212,000 dollars. The previous pastor had built the rectory, but he also left this enormous debt. I stayed there for eleven years, and was able to pay the debt and add some other construction projects, with 60,000 dollars left over. I didn't have to ask the diocese for anything, because the people gave generously. When I turned 70 in 1980, I asked the bishop if I should retire but he told me to stay because the people were happy with me. I stayed, but then I began to have heart problems and had to retire.

The PIME parish in Los Angeles

In 1953 PIME took charge of four parishes in New Mexico (Springer, Cimarron, Roy, Maxwell, see chapter VII). In 1964, PIME returned those parishes to the archbishop of Sante Fe. because every available member was needed to staff the new seminaries which were opening. The original plan had been to have a high-school seminary on the West Coast as well, so a continued presence in that part of the country was important. Father Nicholas Maestrini spoke to the auxiliary bishop of Los Angeles, Timothy Manning, who welcomed him with open arms. He remembered that the missionaries of PIME (the Roman branch[3]) had worked in California

---

[3] The Pontifical Seminary of the Holy Apostles Peter and Paul for the Foreign Missions was founded in Rome by Bishop Pietro Avanzini, according

from the beginning of the century up to 1926, when they were expelled from Mexico (Baja California) by the anti-clerical persecution of the revolutionary government (see chapter VII).

"Many institutes and congregations want to come to Los Angeles," Bishop Manning told Maestrini, "but PIME has precedence." And he assigned us the parish of St. Patrick, which the Salesians were just leaving. Father Dante Carbonari, former missionary in Burma and then in New Mexico and chaplain of the Apostolate of the Sea in the harbor of Los Angeles, was the first PIME pastor. Following his death on January 2, 1972, Fr. Giulio Cancelli (missionary in India) took over, up to his own death on March 18, 1985. Fr. Mark Tardiff was pastor from 1985 to 1987, when he left for his mission assignment in Japan, followed by Fr. Bruno Piccolo until 1991. Thus, PIME cared for the parish for around 30 years.

St. Patrick, situated in the south central area of Los Angeles, followed the course of many national parishes in the States. First it was an Irish parish (thus the name, St. Patrick); then the Irish moved to another area and in the 1940s it became an Italian parish; then, in the 1960s the Italians too moved on, and the area became Black and Hispanic (particularly Mexican).

In 1972, the old parish church, very large but built without anti-seismic reinforcement, was severely damaged by a violent earthquake. The diocese felt that there wasn't much of a future for the parish and decided to

---

to the desire of Pius IX, in 1872. In 1926 Pius XI united it to the Lombardy Seminary for the Foreign Missions in Milan (founded in 1850 by Bishop Angelo Ramazzotti and the bishops of Lombardy). At that time (1926) the title was Institute for the Foreign Missions (of Milan); thus PIME (Pontifical Institute for Foreign Missions), the name of the new missionary institute given by Pius XI, was born.

tear down the church building and construct a large parking area for the school. Thus the school hall became the place of worship. After the death of Fr. Carbonari, the Curia decided to close the parish. Fr. Cancelli, who knew Spanish well and had worked with Fr. Carbonari, went to the archbishop and said: "If you'd like, I will establish a parish for the Hispanic immigrants."

In those years the legal and illegal immigration from Mexico and Central America (especially Guatemala) was becoming a serious problem for the civil authorities and also for the church, given that the poor people in search of work were baptized Catholics, albeit poorly evangelized. Thus, Fr. Giulio Cancelli, a man with a large heart and strong pastoral sense, transformed St. Patrick into a parish for the Hispanics.

Fr. Bruno Piccolo recounts the following:

> One of his customs was to invite seven, eight or nine priests of the area once a month for a meal, to express priestly and fraternal unity, and the chancery liked this very much. Sometimes even the archbishop came for dinner, and Cancelli, a great host, full of stories from his mission days in India, would cook spaghetti and other Italian foods. Fr. Giulio was known and loved in the diocese and when he had to remain alone in the parish because PIME didn't have anyone else to send there, Fr. Joseph Alzugaray, diocesan director for the Propagation of the Faith, went to live with him. He continued to work in the chancery but he lived in the rectory of St. Patrick. A great friend of the missions and of PIME, he assigned many mission appeals to us,

and helped us found the mission center in a house across from the parish. It was started in the late 1970s by Fr. Angelo Bianchi, who had been a missionary in Guinea-Bissau.

At the beginning of 1985, Fr. Pasquale Persico, former missionary in India, went to help Fr. Cancelli, but after only a few months Fr. Giulio died. Fr. Persico remained in Los Angeles up to 1991, when PIME returned administration of the parish to the archbishop, and he then went to the PIME house in Florida for retired PIME missionaries to assist Fr. Nicholas Maestrini.

The PIME mission center in Los Angeles

The presence of PIME in Los Angeles was hampered by a premature death. Fr. Luigi Maggioni (U.S. regional superior from 1976 to 1988) comments:

> Father Angelo Bianchi unfortunately lived only a short time: when he came to America from Guinea-Bissau he was already afflicted by an illness contracted in the mission. He died at the age of 41 on April 18, 1984. He had a great spirit and in a few years he was able to establish good relationships with the diocese, neighboring parishes, friends, and benefactors.
>
> He had a lot of courage: for example, he went to visit the diocesan seminaries, where we had never gone unless we were invited, which never happened. He would arrive with films, books, brochures, the map of Guinea-Bissau, and the doors opened to him; he was able to speak to the clergy and seminarians. Then he became

friends with the editor of the *National Catholic Register*, who published three articles on Guinea-Bissau, which drew many responses from readers all over the country. The people at the newspaper said that they had never experienced such a response as that received by this series of articles.

Fr. Bianchi also used the mass media for promotion and created a PIME Women's Guild. Fr. George Berendt, who had been a missionary in Japan, also went to the mission center in Los Angeles for a few years, assisting the Catholic Vietnamese community on the West Coast, from which would come some missionary vocations for PIME.

In the 1970s and 1980s there were other missionaries who worked in Los Angeles and San Francisco: Fr. Francis Ricciardi and Fr. Aldo Vinci. Fr. Ricciardi, who had been a missionary in Hong Kong, died July 11,1990. Fr. Aldo Vinci, a missionary from Myanmar, was chaplain of the "Pro Sanctitate" movement and lived in the parish of the Minimi Franciscans in Los Angeles. He died December 11,1990. Father Vinci was a great promotor; he spoke much of the missions. He helped in the parish and collected donations to send to his mission of Kengtung.

After the death of Father Cancelli, from 1985 to Easter of 1988, the pastor was Fr. Mark Tardiff (now in Japan). Then Fr. Bruno Piccolo became the pastor, returning to Detroit in 1991 to work with the PIME college seminarians. Administration of the parish was then returned to the archdiocese and continues to thrive with a diocesan pastor of Mexican origin, who has attracted many parishioners. Today six Masses are celebrated between Saturday evening and Sunday in the school hall, because the church has never been rebuilt.

PIME continues an occasional presence in California with Fr. Claudio Corti, who goes once or twice a year, to visit the young men with whom he is in contact in regard to vocational discernment (see chapter. VIII). Fr. Pasquale Persico also goes back to St. Patrick parish for several weeks during the year.

CHAPTER VI

THE MISSION AMONG THE MIXTEC INDIANS IN MEXICO

ON THE EVENING OF MAY 1, 1997 I LANDED AT THE INTERNA-tional airport of Acapulco in Mexico, coming from Detroit and Dallas. Father Luigi Maggioni picked me up and brought me to the diocesan seminary where I was given a room for the night. In Acapulco, where tourism reigns, you can meet people from all over the world, including groups of Italians. In fact, someone recognized me: "Aren't you that missionary who speaks about the gospel on television? Did you come here to enjoy the beach?" "No," I answered, "tomorrow we're going into the mountains to visit a mission of the Mixtec Indians."

A week later, returning to Acapulco, I went to look for those Italians. When I found them, I recounted what I had seen, arousing amazement and maybe even disbelief.To these good tourists it seemed impossible that not too far from the heaven-on-earth which is Acapulco with its five-star hotels, pools, the beautiful ocean and white sand beaches, water sports of all kinds and high-class restaurants, there are people that live with very few modern amenities.

The PIME Missionaries among the Mixtecs of Guerrero

Yet, it's true. Leaving Acapulco on the comfortable Panamerican Highway (which traverses the continents from Alaska to Chile), you travel about 80 miles south, to Marquelia and then turn inland along mountain roads, climbing the Sierra Malinaltepec which reaches more than 7,000 feet. Up to San Luis Acatlán, the last village inhabited by Spanish speakers, the road is passable during the day, even if it is a bit dangerous, especially when you encounter another car or truck coming from the opposite direction. Soon after you enter Mixtec land. Traveling by four wheel drive pick-up, we arrived in Yoloxochitl in two hours and then on to Cuancaxtitlán in another hour. The distance is not that great, but the mountain roads are rugged and you need a strong back to withstand the jolting. At times not even the truck can make it, and it is necessary to go on foot or by burro.

The mission entrusted to the PIME missionaries also includes Arroyo Cumiapa, about 20 miles from Cuanacaxtitlán, but there are also other groups of indigenous peoples dispersed throughout mountains, reachable only by footpaths.

How do the Mixtecs live? Isolated, abandoned, despised. They are made to feel ashamed of being indigenous, of not speaking Spanish well, of being poor and undeveloped. What's more, they are divided among themselves: family feuds and revenge killings are not uncommon.

At times we missionaries are asked: "Why do you go to disturb people who live according to nature; they are peaceful and happy." These friends are mistaken, they have a mythical or ideological view of reality. I have seen tribal people isolated in the forests in Mexico and in the Amazon, in Africa, in Burma, in Bangladesh or in Papua New Guinea, and they live a brutal life. Besides being poor, illiterate, hungry and without sanitary means, they are oppressed by their more developed neighbors and often torn apart by internal struggles.

Among the Mixtecs I saw once again the mission's positive impact on the life of the people. The PIME Missionaries and the Mexican Franciscan Sisters of St. Joseph have helped this people elevate their level of life by providing health care, digging septic tanks, and using concrete for houses. Their lives have been bettered through adult literacy programs and assistance for the existing schools, sewing classes for the women. Also, agricultural techniques are improved and, unknown fruits and vegetables and other crops introduced, cooperatives for production and sale of the local commodities set up — all improving their lives.

But the most important significance of this mission among the Mixtecs was explained to me by the archbishop of Acapulco, Rafael Bello Ruiz:

> The arrival of the PIME Missionaries has opened my eyes to the situation of the indigenous peoples, a problem to which I admit we gave little attention. Today in Mexico we are recognizing that a large part of the population is living in inhuman conditions, cut off from the modern world. When the PIME Missionaries came to this diocese, I felt like I had won the national Lottery and I thank the Lord that He has sent them. I am enthusiastic about the way PIME works in my diocese. I speak to my priests and seminarians about it and I want them to go to visit them so that they can see the situations that we have in the diocese, so that they can feel responsible and understand just what it means, in practice, to have a missionary spirit.

"This is real mission ad gentes, like in India"

There are about 17–18 million indigenous groups in Mexico, with 56 separate languages. They make up 22 percent of the 80 million Mexicans and little is written about them; while much has been written of Brazilian Amazon Indian groups, of which there are only 300,000. Many indigenous groups live in better conditions than do the Mixtecs, but in general they are still marginalized, even geographically. The integration of these minorities into the national life, while maintaining respect for their traditional languages and cultures, is currently a very grave problem. The tourists who go to Acapulco should take three days off from the beach and go into the mountains to see the other face of Mexico and of Latin America in general.

Fr. Steve Baumbusch told me:

> The mission in Mexico was started in the same way as PIME's missions in New Mexico years ago (see chapter VII): to be the missionary expression of the American region of PIME and to give those who desire to be missionaries a place to go to experience authentic mission life, even if only for a week or month. It is also wonderful for us members who work in the United States, to be able to go there to renew our spirit and enthusiasm for direct missionary activity.
>
> I am most happy that we have begun the mission among the Mixtecs during my tenure as regional superior (1989–1995) and that I was able to be the first of us to work there, even if for a brief time. This small mission territory outside of the States, entrusted to our region, has had a

strong positive impact for us American members of PIME. It has given us a stronger sense of identity, helping us to affirm that, though we are small, we are indeed a part of PIME. It has created a new focus for us all, an image of what PIME is in America.

The mission in Mexico is a valuable tool for our vocation recruiting program, which we are trying to rebuild. It has been difficult for us to establish a consistent vocational program here. In the past ten years we have not had anyone working fulltime in this job. Using the fisherman analogy, I like to say that we have good nets, but we have not had anyone to haul them into shore. We do a good job in advertising, reaching many people, but we have lacked the personal contact which will attract people to join us. Now, Fr. Claudio Corti is doing very well in this area (see chapter VIII) and the mission in Mexico helps a lot. In just these couple of years, 20–25 American young people have gone among the Mixtecs with PIME — some only for 10–20 days, others for a month or more. This summer six will go, for various lengths of time. The fruits are positive: they see and live the mission in concrete terms, they come to know PIME, they grow in their desire to devote themselves to God as missionaries for their entire lives.

Father Luciano Ghezzi told me:

The mission in Mexico has galvanized our American fathers and seminarians; it has given a strong sign also to the friends of the American region of PIME. This year three of our seminarians will come for some weeks to Mexico; there are also young people in vocational discernment who come. But there is another issue as well. In the United States, Spanish is by now the second language and according to some statistics in the next ten years the Catholic church in the U.S. will have a majority of Latinos. There are dioceses that already require their priests to learn Spanish. This mission in Mexico is an excellent possibility as a way to become acquainted with the Hispanic language and culture.

Fr. Luigi Acerbi was a missionary in India for 20 years and since 1986 he has worked in the States. He went to Cuancaxtitlán in November of 1996 and has asked to remain there because, he says,

Here I have found again the real mission *ad gentes* which I experienced in India when I was younger. I don't see a big difference, because the Mixtecs lack basic knowledge of Christianity, even if they have been baptized. But then, nobody has taken care of them; they are abandoned, marginalized, and exploited just as my Santal and Oraon tribals have been in Bengal.

We PIME missionaries always want to go to serve the poorest, the least, the most isolated, and the same is true here in Mexico. Thus, I would say that the difficulties of the surroundings, the distances, the poverty, the physical dangers that we meet here on the Sierra Malinaltepec, really aren't very different from the difficult conditions of life that I found in India. For me this type of real mission is characteristic of other PIME missions throughout the world.

Guerrero: the poorest and most violent state in Mexico

Fr. Luigi Maggioni and Fr. Steve Baumbusch, were the first from PIME to go among the Mixtecs. In November of 1992, he went on an exploratory trip to the place and had various meetings with the archbishop of Acapulco, Rafael Bello Ruiz, and other bishops and missionary institutes in Mexico. They readily saw that the mission was necessary. Through the Franciscan Sisters of San Joseph, who work in the PIME houses in Detroit and Newark, Ohio, the bishop offered the mission to PIME.

In October of 1993, Fr. Steve returned to establish PIME's presence in Cuancaxtitlán, joined a month later by Fr. Stefano Andreotti (now a missionary in Hong Kong). They began to work with the Franciscan Sisters of St. Joseph, who had been in the mission since 1978. Others followed, for various periods of time: Frs. Luigi Maggioni, Bruno Piccolo, Edward Miley, Andrew Riley, Claudio Corti, Luigi Acerbi and Luciano Ghezzi. Today the permanent member in the mission is Fr. Luigi Maggioni, with the others coming to assist on a rotating basis, since each one still has other duties to perform in the U.S.

I visited the mission among the Mixtecs in May of 1997. It is composed of three villages: Cuancaxtitlán, or

Cuana for short, (6,000 inhabitants), Yoloxochitl (3,000) and Arroyo Cumiapa (700), as well as various smaller villages dispersed throughout the mountains. Beyond Cumiapa one can travel only by horse or on foot. The region is isolated; it's been only a year that Cuancaxtitlán has had a public telephone line, and it still works only rarely. In the rainy season, the missionaries must walk or ride horses to visit the villages. Agriculture is the only means of sustenance. Corn, beans, peanuts and a few other crops are cultivated. If it rains too little or too much, there is famine and hunger. The fields produce very little; the Mixtec farmer digs a hole in the ground with a stick and drops in the seed. There are no such things as plows or tractors. They carry everything on their heads or on the backs of the burros. Their main tool is the machete, which they use for everything.

In Cuana, as in the other villages, the most ordinary norms of hygiene are not known; there is no water purification nor sewers. The infant mortality rate is very high, especially due to tuberculosis and cholera. Water is scarce for half of the year and the streams that pass through the villages are used for cooking, washing, and bathing. Animals graze near the streams resulting in contamination from animal waste.

Guerrero, with Chiapas and Oaxaca, is considered one of the poorest states in Mexico, despite the fact that its capital, Acapulco, is a modern and rich city. The economic benefits of international tourism go to a few dozen families who own hotels, restaurants, night clubs, transportation companies, supermarkets, etc. The majority of the people live in misery, especially the Indians of the mountains, who can't even come down to the city to find work, because they are recognized and excluded.

The Indians also keep to themselves out of timidity

and an inferiority complex. Often they don't know Spanish, and they don't know how to defend themselves from the contempt and the exploitation of the more developed populations. The government has tried to initiate programs to persuade them to move toward the lowland, where it would be easier to help them and integrate them. But each tribe has its mountain, its own language, its own ancestors and traditions, and so they continue to live apart, except for occasional contacts in the markets.

The daily newspaper *Excelsior* of Mexico City, the most important of the country, has published a series of articles on the state of Guerrero, in which unbelievable data are found[1]. The illiteracy rate in the mountain regions is more than 60 percent; many have no birth certificate, and so their very existence is not recognized by the state; 85 percent of the population is considered to be "in a state of extreme poverty"; there is massive malnutrition, and in times of famine 50 to 100 people a day die from hunger. This poverty gives rise to violence. The state of Guerrero is "in a more explosive situation than that of Chiapas, a time bomb that the government is trying to deactivate," but only by militarizing the region without attacking the deeper causes of the poverty — ignorance, isolation, lack of health facilities and schools, etc.

A local joke says that the Mixtec Indians will never go to hell, because they are already experiencing it here on earth; and even if they have to spend some time in purgatory, they won't think it's too bad.

---

[1] *"Miseria, Violencia y Armas, Peligro Latente en Guerrero"* in *Excelsior,* April 16, 1997, pp.1,10, 12,31-A; *"Pobreza extrema de 85 por ciento de personas en la montaña de Guerrero,"* in *Excelsior* April 17,1997, pp.1,10, 38.

"With no attention from the state, it's every man for himself"

Fr. Luigi Maggioni says that the PIME Missionaries found Cuancaxtitlán in a situation of terrible internal violence. In five years (1991–1995) there had been 80 killings in this village of around 6,000 inhabitants due to family feuds, revenge, robberies and battles between rival gangs. Many times, especially in the beginning, the missionaries heard confessions in which a person would say, "I killed a man," as if he were saying, "I killed a chicken." Fr. Maggioni adds:

> Everyone lives in fear. Nobody intervenes, nobody says anything. There are often revenge killings, robberies along the road, people stopped and stripped of everything and murdered if they resist. And if anyone knows who the criminals are, they don't say anything. Even if they are arrested, they can pay the judges or the jailers, then come out and seek revenge on the one who accused them. Now the assaults have decreased, in part because of our presence as missionaries, but up to a little while ago the situation really did seem to be like a wild West movie. People would be stopped along the road by masked bandits, who would take all their money and sometimes violate the women.

The situation has definitely improved with the presence of the PIME Missionaries and the Mexican Franciscan Sisters of St. Joseph. There is a new spirit of reconciliation felt by all. A woman, who accompanied me to celebrate the Mass in front of a large cross in the village square, said to me:

Before the fathers came, nobody in our village would go out of their own house. We were afraid of one another; there had been so many killings, revenge attacks and brutal robberies. Today you see the children playing out in the open. This is something new. Before, we stayed inside as much as possible.

Fr. Maggioni adds:

The first months that we were here, when you went out on the street, you didn't see anyone; if you did meet someone, they avoided you, not even responding to your greeting. Now the people are out in the streets; they speak to one another, even smile at others they don't know, and the children can run and play. A new atmosphere has been created and the violence has greatly diminished. And then, nobody would ever hurt the nuns and the priests; so, when we go out in the pickup, everyone wants to come with us, because they know that they will be safe. This tendency toward violence comes from isolation, from extreme poverty and from the lack of police, law and justice. There is enormous corruption in the structures of the state. The one who pays the most is always right, so people take justice into their own hands. In one week, I buried four victims of revenge killings. It should be said that in general these are good people — welcoming, friendly, generous with the little that they have, simple in their faith; but they are accustomed to seeking justice on their own and this brings about family feuds which go on for years and years.

I'll give you one example that I have seen myself. A good man, a practicing Catholic, had two sons who went to work for a landowner in another village. But this owner never paid them, didn't even give them anything to eat. They tried to ask for their salary but never got anything. One night, they killed the owner with an ax. They admitted it to me very calmly: "We killed him and then escaped." There is no state involvement, so each one seeks justice on his own; then they take off, not for fear of the police, but for fear of the revenge of the victim's relatives. The problem of violence in the state of Guerrero is terrible. Once a young man came to ask my advice: "Padre, I saw the ones who killed so and so. What should I do? If I go to tell the police, they will know right away who reported it." I told him: "Be careful that they don't kill you too."

Chindeetanyo: Working Together

The work done by PIME in a few years is significant from all points of view. Without doing anything extraordinary, they immediately gave concrete examples of how to improve living conditions and the Mixtecs have imitated them. For example, they built the Sisters' house and the second floor of the mission house, the church in Cuana and now the chapel in Arroyo Cumiapa with brick and concrete. Fr. Maggioni relates the following:

> When we arrived, the houses were made of mud; there were practically no houses made of bricks. Now there are many of them, just like the buildings of the mission. These projects also provide jobs for many and training for anyone who wants to learn. On the mission grounds we have dug septic tanks and made the first real hygienic toilet system in the village (the government has been talking about this for years, but has done nothing). The people see this and come to ask us to teach them to do the same. Now many houses in Cuana have a real bathroom. We have made an incinerator where we burn our trash, rather than throwing it out on the street, where dogs and pigs come by to eat it, and then letting the rain wash away the rest. Now they understand that this contaminates the water of the stream that passes by Cuana, and they are making incinerators too. We are building a public washing area for the women, who up till now have been washing their clothes in the stream with contaminated water. Now their washing water comes from several wells that have been dug.
>
> For several months the mission has been paying a physician from San Luis Acatlán to come to Cuana five days a week to run a dispensary in the mission house, helped by Sister Judith, who distributes the medicines which come from Italy and the United States. The more serious cases

are taken to the clinic in San Luis Acatlán. This is the first real health care they've ever had in this area. This young physician, a good Catholic, has a niece who is also a doctor and a wife who is a nurse. They run a small pharmacy and four-bed clinic in San Luis Acatlán. They do great work, for which we pay about 600 dollars a month.

Another project already underway is the sewing school run by the sisters in two groups, one made up of married women and the other for young girls. They teach how to cut the cloth, to sew, to make and mend clothes. They wear clothes here until they fall to shreds, because they don't know how to repair them.

All these projects have begun with the collaboration of *Chindeetanyo*, a committee which we just recently established. It is a Mixtec word which means "Working Together". The committee meets to discuss the needs of the village, decide upon projects and plan for the necessary work . We are at their service; we help and assist, but we want them to reach shared decisions on their own. It is a new experience: they have regular meetings, the secretary writes a report, the president and the administrator lead, and everyone participates. The meetings are not held in the church, because we want to make clear that this is a lay body. Rather, they are held at the *Comisaria*, the town square where people commonly assemble.

Chindeetanyo is a concrete example of village democracy and also of community growth. Now they have decided, in addition to other projects, to create a community park of about 1,500 square yards, to provide a place for relaxation, family gatherings and a playground for the children, as well as to educate the people to respect the trees, plants and other aspects of nature. On these mountains they often cut down trees without replanting and burn brushwood for fertilizer. At times fire spreads through the mountains and nobody dreams to do anything about it. But it should also be added: they have no means to stop it.

A bank in the parish of Cuana

In the short week that I spent in Cuana, Yoloxochitl and Arroyo Cumiapa, I saw several other plans for development. Fr. Luciano Ghezzi, who accompanied me on the visit, told me:

We have also started a bank in the parish. Banks do not exist among the Indians; if you want one, you have to go all the way to Acapulco! Ours is open on Saturdays and Sundays; it's not run by the parish, but by the Savings and Loan Cooperative which has its office on the mission grounds. We opened two accounts in a bank in Acapulco. The real value is not in giving interest but in creating the mentality that you don't need to spend all the money you earn right away. The concept of saving is unknown here. If someone earns a little money, that person spends it right away on parties or to buy useless things. The bank is a means of education.

Another project that we are working on is the *granero*. The Mixtecs cultivate corn and sell it right away at a low price because they have no place to store it. Then when they need it, they have to go to the market in San Luis Acatlán and buy it back at a higher price. But how to store this corn? Years ago Caritas financed the construction of a storehouse for grains, but it has never been in operation because no one wanted to take charge of it for fear of being killed by thieves! Now it is being repaired and we will establish some rules for the custody of the grain and respect for community property.

But if we were to list all the development projects started by the parish, we would never finish. For example, we have started to put a table with Spanish books and magazines at the back of the church. Anyone can take one home, read it and then return it. In the beginning nobody took anything; they didn't know what to do with a book or magazine! Then they started to read and now the table is often empty. So we've gathered books and magazines in quantity to distribute, so that each family can get used to having something to read at home, and we are enlarging the mission house to include a large room to become a public library.

We've also been able to provide free books and notebooks for the schools and are beginning a project to help all the children to go to school. Some families don't send them to school because they are too poor. An agency from Rome finances the education of 20 children at 20 dollars a month for each, although the number of needy is much more. With this help, the family can provide their children with books and notebooks and a bit more than the usual corn and beans to eat.

The Indians are marginalized from the national life

Archbishop of Acapulco Rafael Bello Ruiz described to me the situation of his vast diocese (about 20,000 square miles) founded in 1958. For about two and a half million inhabitants, there are only 102 diocesan priests — "of which five are seriously ill or very elderly." There are 12 non-diocesan priests (Franciscans and Conventuals, Mercedarians, O.M.I. and PIME) and 145 religious sisters, most of whom work in the city of Acapulco, with over a million inhabitants.

The church in Mexico has gone through, in our century, long periods of real persecution, which has prevented it from being well organized and establishing its structures (seminaries, churches, parishes) throughout the country. Vast territories and populations have remained religiously abandoned. The bishop himself studied at seminaries in United States and France, because from 1936 until the mid 1950s the seminaries in Mexico were closed.

To this historical situation of persecution must be added the lack of a national consciousness in regard to the presence of the Indians. In the beginning, the

Spanish missionaries had approached the native populations, translating catechisms and books into their languages. Then this practice was lost. The upper classes, in the government and in the church, are of Spanish or Meztizo origin. In the past the Indians couldn't enroll in school, nor enter the seminary or novitiate. Little by little, the indigenous peoples were cut off from national life, from commerce, from culture and political power. They settled, or were forced to settle, in the mountains. Thus they remained isolated and underdeveloped. The evangelization which began two centuries ago has made little progress since.

> Only in the last few years has the presence of the Indians come to the fore, for cultural and political reasons. There have been anthropological and linguistic studies, and the government has started to appreciate the aboriginal Mexican cultures. Also the church is doing its part, but we are still far behind where we should be. I myself, even though I've been bishop here since 1974, have been late in recognizing the situation of the Indians. We never thought of them as distinct peoples; we saw their poverty but not the cultural and linguistic diversity. I have had a really active interest in the Indians for only about five years, from the time that PIME came to my diocese and helped me to become more aware of them. But this awareness is new in all of Mexico.

I saw for myself what the archbishop of Acapulco was saying as I visited some bookstores in Acapulco and Mexico City. I wanted to buy some books on the

Indians of Mexico, but I found almost nothing. Brazil has from 200–300,000 Indians in its Amazon forests and in Mato Grasso and there are many studies and books written on these ethnic groups; you can find them everywhere. Mexico doesn't even know the exact number of Indians it has (the estimates are anywhere from 15, to 20, to 25 million!). In the bookstores you can find highly specialized university studies in the fields of linguistics, anthropology and natural religions, or historical studies on the ethnic groups at the time of the Spanish; but books on the current situation of the Indians in Mexico are rare, and the few that exist are very general, of little descriptive value.[2]

"We Mixtecs need the gospel"

The Mixtec people is one of the most numerous of the indigenous tribes, with more than a million members, spread throughout the states of Guerrero, Oaxaca, Puebla and Morelos. They received the Christian message centuries ago, but in the past their villages were visited by a priest only once a year at best. Before the Franciscan Sisters of St. Joseph arrived in Cuana in 1978, a priest had gone to that area only two times in five years. In the long years of abandonment, the Mixtecs preserved their faith, even if it was mixed with many superstitions. For example, illnesses are believed to have not physical but spiritual causes: curses, sins, or the negative influence of spirits. When there is sickness, before looking for adequate care, they try to find

---

[2]For example, the small book of Lilian Scheffler, *Los indígenas mexicanos* (Ed. Panorama, Mexico, 1997, 152 pages) simply lists the 54 tribes of Mexican Indians according to four anthropological and linguistic groups, devoting two or three pages to each. But it doesn't say how many Indians there are, nor in what kind of conditions they live, nor their relationship with the government and with Mexican society, etc.

out who is to blame, who placed the spell.

> When they come to confess, they don't talk about their sins, but the illness and the misfortunes that they have as a consequence of the sin. They ask pardon for the sin in order to begin feeling better. The Mixtecs, even though they are Catholics, have a somewhat polytheistic belief. They pray to God, the Virgin Mary and the Saints, but mix Christian imagery with pagan divinities. They look to religion for comfort and defense against the hard daily reality they face, and they often resort to various forms of magic.

Ulises Aldama Hernandez has been *comisario*, or mayor, of Cuancaxtitlán three times (for four years each), in 1962, 1976 and then in 1981. He speaks about his people and forcefully expresses the need they have of the gospel.[3]

> My people need the gospel, today more than ever, because, with the modern world that is arriving in our villages through TV, the young people become impatient with family life and don't listen to their parents any more. We don't know how to teach them. Also in the relationship between man and woman we need the gospel, because we men are *machistas:* we believe that our women are inferior, we treat them harshly, we don't listen to the opinion of our wives and we don't take care of our

---

[3]See also the article of the mayor of Cuana: "We Mixtecs need the gospel," in *PIME World*, June 1995, page 3.

126

children, because we say that this is women's work.

We work hard in our fields, but we are not good administrators of what we earn from our work. We spend everything on a party, a marriage, a baptism, without thinking about the future of our family. If we were better Christians, we would also be better citizens, because the foundation of human development is in the love of God for humanity and in a life according to the gospel. We are appreciative of the PIME missionaries and sisters who have come to bring us the gospel, but we desire and we pray to have our own Mixtec priests serve our villages and our families.

I have seen the church being born among the Mixtecs

From the time they arrived among the Mixtecs, the PIME Missionaries have celebrated around 700 baptisms of adults and children and blessed hundreds of marriages. There are strong popular devotions, with processions, ceremonies, novenas, Eucharistic Adoration, veneration of the Blessed Mother and the Saints. With the help of PIME, the people have rebuilt the church of Cuana, almost destroyed by a strong earthquake years ago, and are now doubling the size of the chapel in Arroyo Cumiapa. They have also built the sisters' house and enlarged the mission house. There is now a plan to acquire some houses near the church, to make a center in which to organize all the pastoral activities. Additionally, there is a program of intensive catechesis, bringing people from all the villages to the mission house in Cuana for courses of religious education.

The catechism classes for the children are presented by the three sisters, Zeferina, Juanita and Judith. They are assisted by lay catechists, who are also ministers of the Eucharist and are involved in many other pastoral activities (visits to the sick, etc.). Everything is done on a volunteer basis; these are farmers with families of their own, but they give part of their time to the church. They also translate for the missionaries from Spanish to Mixtec when necessary. Mixtec is a difficult language for which there are no books nor teachers. On the other hand, not all of the people speak Spanish. As the mission continues to develop, it will be more and more necessary for the missionaries to learn the Mixtec language. Religious literature in this language is also needed.

Father Steve Baumbusch describes the spirituality of the Mixtec people in this way:[4]

> The people of Cuana participate in different types of devotions, among which Eucharistic adoration is perhaps the most popular. There are two groups dedicated to the adoration of the Blessed Sacrament, one for the men and one for the women. The men commit themselves to all-night adoration each first Saturday of the month, while the women attend adoration on the fourth of the month during the day. We celebrate the Mass at 6:00 a.m. and we have exposition of the Holy Eucharist; they begin their turns of adoration, and we conclude with benediction and Mass at 6:00 p.m. The opposite schedule is fol-

[4]"Mixtec Spirituality," in *PIME World*, February 1996, pp. 15–16.

lowed for the men's all-night adoration, which begins with Mass at 6:00 p.m., followed by the men taking their turns at adoration and concluding with another Mass at 6:00 a.m. Each group has about 60–70 members, each of whom devotes two hours of prayer in front of the Blessed Sacrament.

In Cuana there are also "evangelization groups" who gather in private homes to listen and reflect upon the Word of God, and to build a community consciousness through common prayer and discussion. I participated in one of these meetings with Fr. Maggioni. In a house made of mud, about 15 people sat on wooden benches, men and women with children in their arms and running all about. A man read a passage of the Gospel in Spanish and in Mixtec; there was a period of silent prayer; and then each one commented on the Gospel passage, some in Spanish, others in Mixtec.

I said something too, but I was sincerely touched, not so much by what was said, but because it seemed like I was participating in the birth of the church, just like in the Acts of the Apostles. There was a spirit of faith, an enthusiasm for the faith, a coming together, in the poverty of their human situation, around the Word of God, that made me think what it must have been like for the great missionary St. Paul when he met with the first Christian communities. There was no St. Paul here of course, but the Spirit was the same as at that time.

CHAPTER VII

PIME MISSIONARIES IN NEW MEXICO AND AMONG THE CHINESE IN CANADA

THE MISSIONARIES OF THE ROMAN BRANCH OF PIME[1] WORKED IN Baja California, Mexico, in Los Angeles and in San Francisco from 1895 to 1926, when, expelled from Mexico by the revolutionary government, they left the United States as well and went as missionaries to China, Bolivia and Argentina. Fr. Joseph Cotta remained in Los Angeles until his death (1931); Fr. Severo Alloero and two others continued to work in the northern part of the mission of Baja California in the thirties, "through the good graces of a less hostile governor," he wrote in a report of that time.

PIME founded the church in Baja California

In Mexico PIME founded the church in Baja California, which received some thirty Italian missionaries in thirty years (1895–1926). The mission of La Paz[2], after the expulsion of the Italians in 1926, was passed to the native clergy formed by our missionaries. The history of this first presence of PIME in Mexico and in the American West was never written down. We know that some tombs of our missionaries can still be found in the

---

[1]See Chapter V, note 4.
[2]La Paz, which was simply a *"missione sui juris,"* became an apostolic vicariate in 1957 and a diocese in 1988.

cemeteries of La Paz and Los Angeles and that some of the churches built by them are still functioning. In 1969, in Mexico City, I met a Comboni missionary who had worked in Baja California; he told me that the missionaries of PIME are well remembered and many signs of their work remain in the diocese.

When Fr. Guido Margutti arrived in the United States in 1946 (see chapter I), he had in mind to open a "home mission" among the Indians, the Blacks or the Mexican-Americans. Thus, PIME would present itself not only as a missionary institute that came to America to ask for economic help, but one also ready to contribute its own missionary work among the peoples most in need of religious assistance and human development.

Fr. Nicholas Maestrini took up the same plan and in February of 1952, after having asked the opinion of various American prelates (Cardinal Mooney, Monsignor DeBarry, Bishop Fulton Sheen, Maryknoll Bishop Raymond Lane and Father Considine), he set out for California. He visited different dioceses offering the services of PIME for a mission among Spanish-speaking immigrants, but he received negative responses.

For 18 months Fr. Dante slept in the sacristy

On the way back to Detroit, Maestrini stopped in Sante Fe, New Mexico to pay a visit to Bishop Edwin V. Byrne, who had been a missionary in the Philippines and had known PIME in Hong Kong and in other countries of Asia. Byrne immediately accepted the proposal of Maestrini and offered him the parishes of the Springer district, which had just been left by Oblates of Mary Immaculate (O.M.I.), who were concentrating their forces in Texas. The General Directorate of PIME in Rome, always cautious about the proposals of the "volcano" Maestrini, initially vetoed the idea on the grounds that we would be overextending ourselves too much. But the following year, after much insistence and many explanations, a positive response arrived.

New Mexico is bordered by Mexico, Texas, Arizona and Colorado. It is about the size of Italy, but with only about 1.5 million inhabitants. Called "the land of enchantment," in reality it is one of the poorest states in America, relatively underdeveloped in the "continent of abundance" that is the United States. New Mexico is also "the land of contrasts": from arid prairies to fertile pastures, from snow and forest-covered mountains to deep valleys and canyons; and the people of low income and lifestyle together with a few large landowners with endless stretches of territory.

On July 15, 1953 Fr. Luigi Colombo arrived in New Mexico from Detroit to take over the parish of Springer with nine missions to care for in a vast territory: Cimarron, Eagle's Nest, Maxwell, Miami, Koheler, Palo Blanco, Tinaa, Colmor and Farley. In August of 1953, Fr. Dante Carbonari, having been expelled from Burma, came to help Fr. Colombo and the parish was divided in two, with Fr. Dante settling in Cimarron, where there was a chapel but no rectory. Fr. Dante put a cot in the sacristy and slept next to the Lord for 18 months. But the sacristy was too small to serve as bedroom, kitchen, dining room and parish office. Finally a good Catholic family offered the missionary a room for his office and brought him food every day.

The situation of poverty would have discouraged anyone. In Cimarron, at the first Sunday Masses there were a total of just a few dozen people. Fr. Carbonari preserved in his diary the results of the Sunday collection: Cimarron, 14 dollars; Eagle's Nest, 10 dollars, Maxwell, 8 dollars; Koheler, 6 dollars. In human terms this meant hunger for the priest. Who could have blamed him if he had run away. Of course Fr. Dante remained.

Meanwhile, in March of 1954, Fr. Mario Venturini arrived and settled in Maxwell and then, in June of the same year, Fr. Rinaldo Bossi (another one of those expelled from Burma), became pastor in Roy, 40 miles from Springer, a parish added by the bishop when he saw that the missionaries of PIME were serious about their commitment. A while later, Fr. Efrem Stevanin, former missionary in Guinea-Bissau, arrived and went to live with Fr. Luigi Colombo in Springer.

From a cool reception to an enthusiastic welcome

The dimensions of the mission district (four parishes) entrusted to PIME in the diocese of Santa Fe were enormous: 90 by 70 miles, bigger than some dioceses. From the very beginning the life of the four missionaries was hard. The people, isolated civilly and religiously, were distrustful; they didn't want to get involved nor to help the priests in any way. Besides not receiving even the basic necessities of life, the moral environment had to be depressing for a priest. Many families had been formed without marriage, the children — many not even baptized — grew up without religious education and without the sacraments. On Friday nights, after everyone received their weekly pay, the bars and dance halls were filled to overflowing.

In Cimarron, Fr. Carbonari began to build the rectory. He acquired a piece of land next to the church and dug the foundation himself. For three months, the people passed by the church and saw the father working, but nobody stopped to give a hand or to ask what he was doing. Then, little by little, seeing that the father was serious about staying, the people began to help and the rectory was finished, at a cost of 11,000 dollars. Immediately afterwards, construction began on the community center of Cimarron: a parish hall for catechism classes, community meetings, get-togethers, movies, etc.

Meanwhile, Fr. Dante was visiting the families and the sick, even those quite distant and abandoned; he took care of the children, convalidated marriages, began regular catechism classes; he initiated the Cursillos, a three-day retreat and course of studies; he founded the Immaculate Conception Clinic, a first aid station and medical clinic in a region without physicians (the nearest was 25 miles away) and health care; he was able to find a nurse, belonging to a group of lay missionaries who settled in Cimarron, and a Catholic doctor who would come once a week from Springer.

The people passed from coldness to welcome and enthusiasm. They had never seen someone so concerned about their human condition and so ready to help them in concrete ways. The same story was repeated in the other parishes.[3] The PIME missionaries remained ten years in New Mexico (1953–1963): they built churches and rectories, Catholic schools and medical dispensaries; they brought in sisters and lay missionaries; above all they gave to the Catholics a sense of unity and the importance of faith in one's personal and family life.

When Fr. Carbonari arrived in Cimarron in 1953, the Catholics had almost disappeared. In 1961, when he left the parish,[4] 750 practicing parishioners were registered.

---

[3]Fr. Carbonari is the only one to leave an account of his mission.

[4]Father Dante Carbonari went to Los Angeles in that year as diocesan chaplain of the Apostolate of the Sea and then became pastor at St. Patrick (see Chapter VI).

In 1964 PIME returned administration of the four parishes to the archbishop of Santa Fe, having fulfilled the task it had been called to do, that is, to refound the church there. Thirty-three years later, in 1996, Frs. Raffaele Magni and Claudio Corti returned to those same parishes in New Mexico to make a video documentary on the work of the PIME missionaries. To their amazement they found two streets named after our fathers and many people who thanked them for what PIME has done: "Your missionaries have left a great memory. The beautiful Christian community that you see today is the fruit of their work and of the spirit that they have given to us all."

From China to Toronto, Ontario, Canada

PIME has a long history of work among the Chinese people: in Hong Kong since 1858 and in mainland China since 1869. In the years 1948–1955, five bishops and around 150 missionaries of PIME were expelled, often after "popular trials," condemnation, torture and imprisonment. In the century in which the missionaries of PIME evangelized China, they founded the following dioceses:

In the region of Guangdong: Hong Kong.

In the region of Honan: Kaifeng, Nanyang, Loyang, Chumatien, Weihweih, Kweiteh, Chengchow, Sinyang, Sinsiang.

In the region of Shensi: Hanchung and Hingan.

PIME not only founded these 12 dioceses in China, but also contributed to the evangelization of the Chinese continent with the blood of its members. Blessed Alberic Crescitelli was tortured and killed in 1900 during the anti-Christian persecution of the Boxers. Pope

Pius XII, while beatifying him it 1951, described his martyrdom as "one of the cruelest in Christian history". There were also six other PIME martyrs in China and two in Hong Kong.[5]

Today PIME works among the Chinese in Taiwan (diocese of Kaoshiung) and in two missions for Chinese immigrants in London, England and Toronto, Canada. The mission of Toronto, while directly under the supervision of PIME's general directorate in Rome, for practical purposes is a part of the U.S. Region of PIME. I visited it in May of 1997 with the U.S. regional superior, Fr. Bruno Piccolo.

There I met Fr. Nicola Ruggiero, missionary in Hong Kong for 40 years, from 1950 to 1989, when he came to Canada to establish the mission among the Chinese. Fr. Nicola, who had also been regional superior in Hong Kong in the eighties, is much appreciated because he speaks Cantonese[6] very well. In the many visits that I have made to Hong Kong throughout the years, whenever I spoke with the confreres of PIME about the difficulty of learning the Chinese language, they always praised Fr. Ruggiero because, they said, "when he speaks Chinese, if not for the white face, you would think he was Chinese himself, so fluent is he in the language." I asked Nicola if this is true, and he responded:

> For some reason, Chinese came easily to
> me from the very beginning. I have a good

---

[5]The stories of these martyrs can be found in *Crimson Seeds* (PIME World Press, 1997)

[6]Throughout most of China, Mandarin, the language of Beijing, is spoken, while in the southern region of Kwangtung (Guangdong), with around 65 million inhabitants, the written Chinese is the same, but with completely different tones and pronunciation. This is the Cantonese language, spoken also in Hong Kong.

ear and good pronunciation, and the tones never gave me any problems. The Chinese have a tonal language, If you like music and singing, and you have a good memory, it's not that difficult. I took classes, but I really learned it well by speaking with the people, so my Chinese is rather colloquial, and the people like that. The Chinese pastor of the Cathedral of Hong Kong once told me: "When you preach in Chinese, it makes me think about the gift of tongues given by the Holy Spirit, because you speak just like a native, and this can't come from study alone." Bishop Lawrence Bianchi, the last PIME bishop of Hong Kong[7], always wanted me to go with him when he visited the parishes or administered Confirmations. He had trouble speaking Chinese, so I preached the sermon for him: he would tell me what he wanted to say, and then I would speak in his name.

Four Chinese parishes in Toronto

Canada is home to around 800–900 thousand Chinese immigrants, 50 percent of which are in Toronto (30 percent in Vancouver). Canada has grown from a population of 15 million in the early eighties to about 30 million today because it has opened its doors to many foreigners, especially the Chinese and Vietnamese. After the English and French, the third largest ethnic group is

---

[7]Lawrence Bianchi (1899–1983), missionary in China from 1923 to 1969 and bishop of Hong Kong from 1949 to 1969. See Piero Gheddo's book, *Lawrence Bianchi of Hong Kong*, Catholic Truth Society, Hong Kong, 1992, 216 pages.

the Italians (more than a million) but in a few years, the statistics say, they will be overtaken by the Cantonese-speaking Chinese, who come for the most part from Kwangtung. It is for this reason that PIME responded to the request of the Canadian bishops to assign two missionaries from Hong Kong, Nicola Ruggiero and Benito Bottigliero, to Toronto (the latter has since gone to London to open another mission for the Chinese).

Fr. Nicola arrived in Toronto in 1989 and for three years he stayed with a Chinese priest in a non-territorial Chinese parish. Then, in December of 1992, he began a new parish in Richmond Hill, named in honor of Blessed Agnes Tsao Kouying, virgin and martyr during the Boxer rebellion at the beginning of the century. Among the Chinese immigrants of Toronto around 12–15 percent are Catholic. There are three parishes serving them: one in the middle of city, in the old "Chinatown," by now almost abandoned because most of the parishioners have moved out of the city; one in Scarborough (the most frequented, where the Mandarin-speaking Chinese attend); and that of Ruggiero in Richmond Hill, where Cantonese is spoken. A fourth parish is being planned, given the number of conversions and the interest that these immigrants have in the Catholic church.

On Sunday evening, May 18, 1997, about 450–500 Chinese parishioners gathered at the Century Palace Chinese Restaurant to celebrate the feast of Blessed Agnes. Fr. Ruggiero introduced me to many families who emigrated from Hong Kong in recent years, and who knew the PIME missionaries well in that English colony, which passed to China on July 1, 1997.

It was a beautiful evening, with the classic fifteen-course Chinese meal, speeches, games, songs and music, comic skits, and gifts for the guests. In that joyous and festive gathering, I understood concretely the value of the work done by Fr. Nicola. In a few years, he has established a solid parish among the Chinese, creating a great spirit of community and attachment to the church.

Mass, sermons and catechesis in Chinese

I asked Nicola how many members there are in his parish.

> I don't have exact figures, but there are about 660–670 registered families, with 4–5 members per family. For Sunday Mass there has never been less than a thousand in attendance. About 30 persons help me with catechism, for both the children and adults. We baptize more adults than children because the conversions are numerous. There is a good response to the initiatives of the church, because religion is a strong factor in the self-identity and unity among these Chinese immigrants, who do not have an easy life here — adapting to a foreign country is difficult for anyone. That's why they like to stick together, and if a priest speaks Chinese like them, they come from all over.

Is the catechism taught in Chinese or in English? "In Chinese," Fr. Nicola answers.

> The Mass and sermons are also in Chinese, except one Sunday Mass in English. The children who go to school learn English, but they speak Chinese at home. The Canadian government wants to preserve the different national languages and cul-

tures, and every Saturday in the parish there is a free Chinese language class offered by the government. Here is the reason the parish is important for the Chinese: if we don't give Christian formation in their language and in a community that respects their culture and traditions, they will feel distant from the church and will take up other forms of religiosity.

How do the Chinese live in Toronto? What work do they do?

Often they live on what they have earned or continue to earn in Hong Kong. Many, especially in Richmond Hill, go back and forth to Hong Kong 10 or 12 times a year and they'll continue to do business in Hong Kong as long as possible. I think that out of ten families in my parish, six or seven are in this situation. Others instead have sold everything in Hong Kong and now they regret it.

A good number of the Chinese try to establish themselves here in Canada; they look for work, but it is not easy to find it, except for the young people. With what they brought from Hong Kong they begin professional, commercial or industrial activity in Canada. The younger ones are ready to do any type of work, often only parttime, as a means to pay for their studies: manual labor, in the restaurants and markets, in the kitchens, etc. In general, the Chinese families are not in economic distress, but the current situation in Canada is not the best; the 'welfare state' is in crisis. You read in the newspapers that 40,000 government employees could be laid off. Thus, also for the Chinese it is a difficult challenge to establish a secure life in Canada.

The House of the Lord of Heaven

When was the parish of Blessed Agnes started?

The first Mass was celebrated on the feast of Saint Nicholas (December 6) in 1992, but the official institution of the parish came on February 26, 1993. I began in a Catholic school that allowed us to use their theater for Mass and meetings and some classrooms for catechism. Near the school I bought a small house with the help of the diocese, where I have a chapel in which I celebrate daily Mass with a few parishioners who live nearby; it also contains the parish office with the secretary and some rooms for small meetings.

At the end of this year we will begin construction on the new church, already approved by the government, on a lot donated by the Archdiocese of Toronto. We will call it *Tin Chue tong,* "The House of the Lord of Heaven (*Tin* = Heaven; *Chue* = Lord; *tong*= House). It will be a beautiful church with a seating capacity of 620, a basement hall for 550 persons, and two floors in the rear for the rectory, offices and parish activities; all surrounded by a large parking lot. I have already saved a good amount in recent years for this construction, but it will certainly not be enough. But I know that when the work begins, the Chinese will help all they can.

The parish of Blessed Agnes Tsao Kouying is fully functioning, even if it doesn't yet have its own property. Christ the King Catholic School is quite large and provides all the space needed, beyond that which is found in the little house where Fr. Nicola lives. He is assisted by Fr. Angelo Villa, who lives in Detroit but comes each weekend to help out.

I was amazed to see that the majority of those participating at Mass and in the parish meetings were young people; 85 percent of the Chinese Catholics registered in the parish of Fr. Ruggiero are less than 50 years of age. The parish has many youth activities, especially the Scouts and Catholic Action, but parish life is fundamentally based on catechism and religious education by all possible means.

Good possibilities for PIME in Canada

Fr. Ruggiero tries to give a missionary flavor to his parish. "PIME is solely a missionary institute," he says, "and everywhere we go we must bring this spirit and give the local church concrete testimony of how to embody it in the local situation." Fr. Nicola has a beautiful project in mind, but unfortunately PIME does not currently have sufficient personnel to carry it out.

The plan would be to establish a PIME mission center in Toronto, like the one in Detroit. Not to do the same things as Detroit (for example produce a magazine, books and video-cassettes), but to establish a center to stimulate vocations, prayers and aid for the missions. The Canadian church, like that of the U.S., needs to express its missionary identity and character.

Fr. Nicola has already started a group of "Friends of PIME"; he distributes the literature of the institute and solicits prayers for the missions. He dreams of the day when there will be PIME mission center next to the parish, able to inspire the entire diocese and Canadian church with the missionary ideal.

I had dinner with Fr. Evasio Pollo, a seminary classmate of mine who has been a diocesan priest in Canada for 34 years. He told me that Canada, and especially Toronto, offers good possibilities for a missionary institute of Italian origin already present in the neighboring United States. Also in Canada there is a real crisis in terms of the family and priestly and religious vocations. But percentage wise, there are more Catholics in Canada than in the U.S. (a little less than 50 percent as opposed to 25 percent).

CHAPTER VIII
PIME IN NORTH AMERICA TODAY

WHAT IS THE SITUATION OF PIME IN NORTH AMERICA TODAY? The institute has 21 priests and one brother in North America. One of the priests is in Canada, where he works with the Chinese immigrants, assisted by another PIME missionary who joins him for the weekend. One priest is in Mexico working among the Mixtec Indians (various others go to help on a rotating basis); the rest live in the United States. Two are 89 years old and both of them are still quite active (Frs. Nicholas Maestrini and John Boracco); three others are over 80 (Charles Sala, Dominic Rossi and Bro. Anthony Testori), and still others are between 70 and 80 (Casto Marrapese, Nicola Ruggiero, Luigi Acerbi, Edward Miley, Pasquale Persico). The youngest are Claudio Corti (30), Steve Baumbusch (40), Giorgio Paleari and Jim Coleman (both 47).

The American fathers are distributed thus in the missions: three in Japan (Kenneth Mazur, Francis Mossholder, Mark Tardiff), one in India (Francis Raco), one in Bangladesh (James Fannan), one in Papua New Guinea (Phillip Mayfield), one in the Brazilian Amazon (Dennis Koltz) and a student in Rome (Tim Sattler, formerly in the Amazon). Father Sandy Garzarelli, of the Archdiocese of Philadelphia is an associate of PIME who is working in Papua New Guinea.

There are three American students at PIME's theological seminary in Monza, Italy (one of whom, Guy Snyder, is a deacon), and five in the College Formation Community in Detroit. Fr. Ken Mazur, missionary in Japan, says:

> We Americans in PIME are few, and we will probably never be very many. The times of many vocations are perhaps over, at least as far as we can tell today. Fr. Maestrini dreamed of having a hundred American missionaries. But PIME in America is important for the institute, even if we are few. The number of Italian missionaries is decreasing also.

The superior general of PIME, Fr. Franco Cagnasso, wrote in his letter to the American friends of PIME, on the occasion of our fiftieth anniversary in this country:

> We are a small presence in the American church, but nowhere in the Gospel is it said that we must be large and powerful to have meaning! If we accept our condition with joy, rather than with frustration, certainly we will see fruits of love, faith and hope among and around us. We are living in a time of major cultural and religious changes. Nobody can foresee how the church in the U.S. will be in the next 15 or 20 years as regards vocations. We are part of this change and we live it with faith. God continues to bless his people.[1]

---

[1]"Dear Friends," in *PIME World*, April 1997.

PIME has seven houses in North America:

- Detroit (Michigan): Regional Headquarters; College Formation Community; ministry in various parishes; Mission and Promotion Center (where the magazine *PIME World* is produced); nine priests and one brother;
- Mt. Clemens (Michigan): the Italian parish of San Francesco: one priest (assisted by another from the regional house);
- Newark (Ohio): the former high-school seminary, now used as center for retreats and meetings, with various missionary awareness activities and ministry in local parishes; five priests;
- Wayne (New Jersey): center for the vocational recruiting program; local pastoral assistance; two priests;
- Tequesta (Florida): house for rest and rehabilitation; missionary promotion and local pastoral assistance; two priests;
- Toronto (Ontario, Canada): the Chinese parish of Blessed Agnes Tsao Kouying in Richmond Hill, one priest (assisted on weekends by one from the Detroit);
- In Mexico: the mission among the Mixtec Indians at Cuanacaxtitlán (Archdiocese of Acapulco); one priest on a permanent basis (assisted by others on a 2–3 month rotation).

The mission center in Detroit

The mission center in Detroit is the heart of the missionary promotion activity of PIME in North America. Here *PIME World* magazine, mission videos, and vocational literature are produced. It is also the headquarters for such programs as the Foster Parents Mission Club, Leprosy Relief Society, Native Seminarians, and Mission Chapels, as well as fund-raising events such as the Knights of Charity Dinner and PIME Golf Day. I interviewed the current director of the mission center, Fr. Bruno Piccolo, who is also the U.S. regional superior of PIME:

> The mission center currently has twelve employees and we are now involved in hiring a development director, an expert in public relations who would oversee our promotional activities, expand our mailing list, create new initiatives, modernize the computer programs, and so on.
>
> In regard to the priests, we have the minimum number involved: I am the director of the center and also regional superior; Fr. Steve Baumbusch is rector of the College Formation Community, treasurer of the U.S. region and also works in the center for public relations activities. Thus, almost all of the work is done by the lay employees, and they do it well; they are men and women inspired by the missionary ideal, many of whom have worked with us for years. The center has various departments:
>
> 1. Publications, with editor-writer Paul Witte and editorial assistant Peggy Fleming: they prepare PIME World magazine, books, brochures, advertisements, public relations pieces, etc.; Peggy also administers the Native Seminarian program, in which seminarians in the missions are sponsored by benefactors here (147 seminarians from 13 countries).
>
> 2. The Leprosy Relief Society, administered by Barbara Rubaie, who has been with us for thirty years. She receives applications from leprosy centers in the mis-

sions, solicits sponsors for them and channels the funds received, and publishes a newsletter for the benefactors. At the end of January we make an appeal through various diocesan and national newspapers on the occasion of World Leprosy Day. Barbara also coordinates the Knights of Charity Dinner.

3. The Foster Parents Mission Club, through which around 5,000 children in 23 centers in the missions have been 'adopted'. Alice Marino is the director. She is assisted by Maria Biernacki, Betty Burski and Eve Gornowicz, has also been with us for more than 30 years, and has a wonderful personal relationship with benefactors and missionaries. She also publishes a newsletter and is always in search of new sponsors. In October of each year the center sends out a Needy Children Appeal letter with photos and stories of poor children. The contributions received are distributed to missions with the greatest need.

4. The office manager and controller is Bob Rawlings: he takes care of personnel issues, office procedures, evaluations, salaries, and the financial accounts of the center.

5. My secretary, Louise Wright, also assists Fr. Steve with the finances of the region, and handles contacts with the missions and the missionaries, as well as many other administrative duties (insurance claims, travel arrangements, etc.)

6. Don Kuester is the building manager, handling the maintenance of the house and vehicles. He also is the coordinator of the Golf Day fund-raiser and alumni relations.

7. Eddie Burski (with a seniority of over 35 years) works in the print shop, producing brochures, newsletters, stationery, etc: all of the ordinary publications which we put out, except for PIME World magazine, for which an outside printer is used.

8. The receptionist, Judy Lentine, answers the door and telephone, maintains the addresses of benefactors, handles mailings, and is the secretary of vocation department. She also organizes parish mission appeals which are preached by all the fathers. In the 1960s and 1970s we had anywhere from 100–150 mission appeals per year; now, because we have fewer priests to preach the appeals, we have only about 50 per year.

9. Finally, the mission center also has an audio-visual department run by Fr. Raffaele Magni, who has established a decent studio at the house. He is helped by Fr. Claudio Corti and Paul Witte. Together they have converted our original mission films into videos and have produced many new videos as well.

All our PIME missionaries are involved in missionary promotion

Speaking with the lay workers of the center and visiting the various departments, I was impressed with the amount of initiatives going on, besides those mentioned above and the others of which we have spoken in preceding chapters. The work is planned, with efficiency and precision, to run throughout the course of the year. "Between Christmas and the first of the year," the director, Fr. Bruno, says, "we have winter holidays, because things really pick up from that time up to the summer. Each month, besides the normal ongoing work, we have special projects or events."

Here is a summary of initiatives undertaken by the center:

> During the summer, we prepare a variety of Christmas cards and we send out a brochure advertising them for sale. Many people like the Christmas cards, and even though we don't make much profit on the sales, they serve as means for people to know PIME and to make new friends. We also prepare a calendar for all our supporters.
>
> In October the Knights of Charity Dinner is held, and this takes a lot of organization and planning, working with a dedicated committee of volunteers. World Mission Day also falls within this month, with a variety of activities: articles in newspapers, making contact with dioceses to arrange mission appeals, preaching, talks, school visits, and similar events.
>
> In November we celebrate a "victory dinner," a banquet in honor of the Golf Day committee. These men work hard for several months organizing the June golf outing, and on this occasion, we invite them and their wives to a thank-you dinner during which we update them on the mission work they so generously support.
>
> In March, we send out an appeal for

the Novena to Our Lady of Confidence. People respond with offerings and prayer requests, for which we celebrate a novena of Masses in our chapel.

Besides the center in Detroit, the PIME fathers in Newark, Wayne, and Tequesta also engage in missionary promotion activities. One of these is the cultivation of the Mission Guilds, groups of lay Catholics (men and women) that gather together to pray for the missions, and organize fund-raising activities. These guilds were first started in connection with PIME's seminaries in Michigan, Ohio and New Jersey, and still endure today, although in smaller numbers.

In Newark, Fr. Jim Coleman coordinates the PIME Prayer Partnership, a program in which missionaries in the field are united in prayer with the faithful in North America. Fr. Jim sends out a newsletter to the participants and seeks new partners among our missionaries and among the faithful.

In Tequesta, Florida Frs. Nicholas Maestrini and Pasquale Persico have organized small groups of friends, and produce the newsletter "A Window on the World" to keep people informed of the situation of the missions.[2] They are able to send a substantial amount

---

[2]In the mid-seventies, Fr. Maestrini founded *"Il Circolo"*, also known as the "Italian Cultural Association," with the purpose of exposing Americans to the Italian culture (language, art, music, literature), especially those of Italian descent. The Circle has been very successful in this regard, with many initiatives that continue today (language and music lectures concerts, reading and comments of Italian authors, scholarship programs, etc.). Fr. Maestrini is known as a priest and missionary, and often speaks to different gatherings about the missions. The house in Tequesta was originally founded as a place for retirement and rest (including those coming from missions such as the Amazon). It is used by some for short vacations, but in general missionaries do not retire; they continue to work up to the end. Thus, Tequesta has become a house of missionary promotion.

of support to the missions each year.

As can be easily seen, PIME in North American is quite active in missionary promotion, not only with institutional initiatives, but also with personal ones. Visiting the houses of PIME in the States, I was impressed to see that the older missionaries also cultivate friendships, write to benefactors, preach mission appeals, etc. In short, they are always soliciting help and prayers for the missions. Nobody remains inactive. For me, this a sign that the spirit of the American region of PIME, manifested initially by Fr. Guido Margutti and Fr. Nicholas Maestrini, has been from the very beginning totally dedicated to the missions and to priestly ministry.

PIME publications

Since 1990 the magazine *PIME World* (formerly *Catholic Life*) and the publications of PIME have been directed by Paul Witte. Married and the father of two, Paul was a lay missionary with his wife for nine years in Colombia (1969–1978) and then for another ten years in Venezuela (1979–1987). His married daughter lives in Mexico where she is doing social work, and his married son, still in school, intends to do community development in a needy area of the world.

Paul Witte replaced Bob Bayer, who directed the PIME publications for almost 30 years. Both men are highly skilled and filled with missionary spirit; they have brought the magazine to a high level of journalistic excellence and missionary identity. It is an exclusively missionary magazine, and for this very reason it has a strong impact among the readers.

PIME World, with a circulation of about 26,000 copies, presents a good image of PIME and is sent to anyone who collaborates with or helps the missions.

The magazine has a good exchange of correspondence with the readers, who react positively to the articles and to the requests of the missionaries. Its contents are essentially the presentation of missionary life and of the situations that missionaries face in the non-Christian world.

Paul says that, in terms of news from the missions, much depends upon the specific mission area and the missionaries' knowledge of English: "We get letters and articles from the PIME members in English speaking countries of Asia (India, Bangladesh, Burma, the Philippines, etc.), but almost nothing from Africa or Brazil." For this reason they translate articles from PIME's publications in Italy, with which there is a good relationship: exchange of articles and photos, translation of books from Italian, etc.

The publications department of the Detroit Center also produces various newsletters, such as that of the Foster Parents Mission Club, the Leprosy Relief Society, and the PIME U.S.A. Region. They also print vocational material sent out to the hundreds of young people who write expressing a desire to engage in vocational discernment, as well as books and brochures on the missions and the activities of PIME in North America, postcards, calendars, etc.

The recruiting activity of PIME in North America

We return now to the highest priority of PIME in North America: missionary vocations. In the 1950s there were many adult vocations, ex-soldiers who had participated in World War II (1941–1945) or the Korean war (1950–1953): quite a few had seen the work of missionaries in South Asia and were attracted by their example. Most of our vocations were ex-G.I.'s, but PIME received some inquiries in this regard. Unfortunately, only a few actually persevered to ordination. Father Maestrini says:

> Several of these were rather emotional vocations not really solidly based. The bulk of our recruiting activity took place in the Catholic schools and parishes. In some years we were invited to speak about the missions in more than 100 Catholic schools. We showed our films, and invited the boys to our "vocation week" summer camp. In the summer of the 1962, for example, more than 300 boys attended our camps. We didn't keep statistics, but I believe that throughout the 1950s and 1960s we were in contact with thousands of young men, many of whom ended up entering diocesan seminaries or other religious congregations; this is a contribution that we have given to the American church.

Toward the end of the 1960s, the vocation boom began to wane, which made the work of recruiting even more difficult, but it was pursued with no less enthusiasm and vigor. The mission center published brochures and books (for example the book *Alive for Others* in 1975), ran vocational appeals in magazines and advertised in Catholic newspapers. In 1975, PIME had six members involved in vocational ministry: two in Detroit, two in Newark (Ohio), and two in Oakland (N.J.).

In 1965, we had two high-school seminaries, the college and the theological seminary. Then, with the closing of the two minor seminaries and the theologate (since 1995, students of theology have gone to PIME's international seminary in Monza, Italy), the number of vocation recruiters decreased and in the 1980s, no vocational promotors were assigned by the region to this task.

In 1992, two newly ordained priests from Italy came to the U.S. to work in the vocation field. Fr. Stefano Andreotti stayed only a short time before moving on to his mission assignment in Hong Kong. Fr. Claudio Corti is currently the only vocational minister of PIME in North America, and he too looks forward to his mission assignment to Thailand in 1998.

With Fr. Claudio Corti in Wayne, New Jersey

I spent four days with Fr. Claudio Corti at the PIME house in Wayne (New Jersey). His parents happened to be visiting from Italy at the time, which was good because the other member who lives in Wayne, Fr. Luciano Ghezzi, was spending time in the Mexico mission. Besides providing company for Fr. Claudio, his parents were also able to keep an eye on the house while he was traveling for mission appeals and to visit those whom he is accompanying on the journey of vocational discernment.

Fr. Claudio participates in regional and national meetings of vocation directors. His opinion is quite positive in regard to the participation of Catholics in the life of the church. For example, the percentage who attend Sunday Mass is just under fifty percent; there is a good response to the initiatives of the church in regard to charitable works and the needs of the parish and diocese; the American culture is religious, or at least not anti-clerical like that of some other countries.

On the other hand, in regard to the role of the American Catholic church in the lives of young people and vocations, the picture is not so positive. The church doesn't attract young people; there are not a lot of activities for them. Catholic teenagers usually go to church up to their Confirmation and then disappear; they return after they've married, when they are raising families of their own.

What to do in order to inspire and encourage vocations? Fr. Claudio is convinced that we need to get information distributed as widely as possible, and then follow up with personal contacts, by letter, telephone and visits. Here are some of the avenues he uses to get the word out:

1. An ad for PIME in *Vision*, an annual religious vocation discernment yearbook, which has articles and advertisements for many men's and women's congregations. It is sent to dioceses, parishes, Catholic schools, priests and nuns, youth associations, and provided free of charge to individuals who request it. PIME has purchased two pages: an article that presents the institute, our charism and the missions in which we work, and a list of the houses in North America, with a reply card for those who want more information.

2. Missionary columns in some Catholic newspapers in the dioceses where PIME is present and known: two times a month in the *The Michigan Catholic* (Detroit); once a month in The *Catholic New York, The Tidings* (Los Angeles), *The Beacon* (Paterson, N.J.) and *The Catholic Register* (Toronto, Canada); and occasionally in other newspapers, such as the national weekly, *Our Sunday Visitor*. The column is called "The Mission Corner" and it contains short stories written by missionaries, including those of Fr. Piero Gheddo, taken from the books he has published about his missionary trips. A coupon follows the article for those who want to know more about PIME, several of which are sent in each month. In addition to the above "advertorials," vocation advertising is done in Spanish and Vietnamese to reach that audience whose mother tongue is not English.

3. Another important source of contact with young people is the activity of the mission center in Detroit, which publishes PIME World magazine and various brochures and newsletters. Fr. Raffaele Magni, assisted by Fr. Claudio has been working hard to produce mission videos, which are sold to interested supporters, or otherwise distributed to friends, Catholic schools, parishes, Catholic bookstores, etc.

4. Fr. Corti says that the internet is also becoming more and more important in regard to spreading information. PIME has several home pages, both in English and Italian. Often young people will come across the pages and then write for more information. Fr. Claudio answers each one and establishes a relationship; after some time, he then visits those who are interested, meeting their families, and beginning to accompany them in their vocational discernment.

What are the fruits of this activity? A few young men have entered our College Formation Community in Detroit, and others continue an active interest. The presence of two young missionaries like Fr. Claudio and Fr. Stefano Andreotti has energized the vocation department in just a short time; the future is filled with possibilities. The difficulty, Fr. Claudio says, is the indecision of young people; many take quite a long time to decide upon their life's work. However, he adds, there are many young people who are full of ideals, wanting to do good in a life spent for others. For this reason, there are many lay missionaries coming from North America, but PIME has not entered this field because of a lack of personnel and structures to form them and send them on mission.

Fr. Edward Miley tells me that in American dioceses it is considered a good percentage to have one student of theology for every thirty active diocesan priests. PIME, he says, is above average in this regard: we have 22 members in North America and three students of theology in Monza. This is a sign that the Lord continues to bless us. Therefore, there should be no pessimism in regard to the future of PIME in North America.

CHAPTER IX

THE MISSIONARY CHARISM OF PIME IN NORTH AMERICA TODAY

AFTER 50 YEARS, WHAT ARE THE CURRENT PERSPECTIVES FOR PIME in North America? The institute is well established in the States: regional headquarters in Detroit, a formation community, a parish, a mission, initiatives for making friends and soliciting support for the missions, a magazine, missionary and vocational promotion, a positive public image.

PIME's general assembly (Tagaytay, Philippines, in 1989) established with clarity that PIME desires to become more and more an international institute. Thus, the old doubts and questions which have delayed our growth in the past are no longer relevant. Today we need to start with things as they are and build an international PIME, one that is truly American and forward looking.

The future of the institute in North America comes from a sincere, reasoned and very concrete response to these two questions, which we PIME members, together with our American friends, must ask ourselves: what has North America given (and what does it continue to give) to PIME? And what has PIME given (and what does it continue to give) to North America, to the North American church? Every marriage is the fruit of love and love comes from meeting one another, from growing mutual acquaintance and attraction and from the mutual give and take of the two parties. Before concrete situations, there are ideal motivations.

The multi-cultural society is the future of humanity

In Detroit, on April 29, 1997, I interviewed Fr. Giorgio Paleari, missionary in Brazil and for the past two years on the formation team of PIME's College Formation Community in the States. His impressions, fresh and lively, and above all the fruit of personal experiences, express very well the response to the question: what does North America give to PIME?

> After 18 years in Brazil, I came to the United States in 1994; I was 44 years old, and the plan was to study English and continue on to Asia. Then I was asked to stay here, first in the theology seminary in Chicago and now in the College Community in Detroit. In Brazil I had formed a negative image of the States: the multinationals, the CIA, the exploitation of poor countries. Instead, the impression that I've had since I've been here is very positive. I'm fascinated by this multi-cultural society, this mixture of races, languages, cultures, religions, customs. In Chicago, 45 languages are spoken. The process of integration is difficult and carries with it a lot of strong tensions, but it's very enriching as well. You perceive that you are entering into a new dimension of life: the multi-cultural society, which is the future of humanity.
>
> I come from Brazil, which is also a multi-cultural and multi-racial country. But in Brazil, except for the Japanese, the other ethnic groups disappear; they don't

maintain their identity. For example, there are many Blacks in Brazil (more than in the United States), but they have no representation on the national level: a bit of folklore and that's it. Maybe it's because Brazil, more poor and less organized than the United States, tends to be less pluralistic: for example, everyone speaks Portuguese. Here in America you constantly hear Spanish, Arabic, Vietnamese, Chinese, Italian, German, etc.

In the big American cities, like Chicago and also Detroit, there are Irish neighborhoods, Italian, Spanish, Vietnamese, Chinese, Mexican neighborhoods. The Mexican areas have everything from Mexico: the shops, the folklore, the religious celebrations, the language. When you go to the Mexican district in Chicago, there's more Spanish than English spoken. The Way of the Cross through the streets of Chicago on Good Friday, with Mexican folklore and popular religiosity is a moving and fascinating ritual. There's nothing like that in Brazil, where the differences tend to be eliminated.

In the States the immigrants maintain their cultural identity and their language, but they consider themselves Americans and are fiercely attached to that identification, each in their own way. Some are here only to study, but little by little they acquire a spirit that integrates them into the society. In my opinion, this is the "American spirit". America is demonized all over

161

the world, but everyone wants to come and live here, and not for the affluence (there are richer countries, or countries in which life is easier), but because it is the country of freedom and of order, in which everyone has an equal possibility of building their future and to be accepted and respected for who they are.

The United States is a mosaic formed of many peoples. Each people group has its own identity, but together they make up the face of America — even though it is an America with many problems and contrasts.

Various languages and cultures in the Catholic church

Fr. Giorgio continues:

This experience in the States has opened up a new world to me, a privileged vision, because it prefigures the future of humanity. For example, there's no denying that strong racism exists, but at the same time you see that Blacks are proud to be American citizens; they live in a tense situation, but every day they move forward in all fields. The Black middle class is well established, and you find African Americans active in all aspects of American society, including top-level positions.

PIME, in becoming international, has much to learn from the United States. I mean that America is a great "school" for us missionaries, the best in the world, to see how to resolve differences, and how the pastoral activity of the church acquires a new dimension of inculturation and change. In the past there have been some tensions between Americans and Italians in PIME, but they are disappearing. We are learning together how to build an international missionary institute, because here you are accepted as you are. Diversity is accepted, not only in the people, but in the ways and styles of living. There is not a unique American cultural model. For me the big issue in America, and in the world, is how to integrate diverse peoples into a single society, while still respecting their diversity; that is, true pluralism, respectful of all.

Also in the religious field, there is a lot of diversity. In general, this is a Protestant country, but there are many other religions, some of which are experiencing great growth. For example, the U.S. is now home to the largest Islamic community outside of the Arab world. Buddhism, Hinduism, and the "new" religious sects are also present.

This creates a great challenge in regard to interreligious contacts and dialogue and brings to the fore the positive and negative aspects of pluralism, becoming a most significant experience for us missionaries.

There was a time when the American Catholic church was a bit closed in upon itself. Then, with the arrival of the new immigrants, especially the Hispanics and Vietnamese, the church became more open, to the extent that it fosters the religious celebrations of these immigrants; there are

Masses celebrated in all languages. The different ethnic groups retain their traditional religious devotions. In the United States, the Virgin of Guadalupe has become a religious symbol known and revered by all. There are some dioceses which require their young priests to learn Spanish in order to assist these Catholics who continue to arrive in great numbers. The American Catholic church is fully engaged in this process of welcoming and integrating Catholics of various languages and cultures.

This is important for PIME, which was born in Milan with the Ambrosian tradition and then began a process of becoming international. A purely Italian missionary institute doesn't make sense in the new world where "globalization" is taking place. I find it difficult to understand the position of those who want to consider PIME as only Italian.

I would say in regard to PIME in North America, even if there were no other activities (and there are many), the lessons of pluralism alone would be enormously enriching for PIME. Here in the College Community in Detroit, we have Anglos, Vietnamese, Brazilian and Italian seminarians; they begin to live together, to understand the differences, to experience the difficulties of inculturation in a multicultural environment. This has been a wonderful experience. Besides the students from Italy and Brazil, we also hosted four Mexican seminarians of the missionaries of Guadalupe, who stayed with us for a year to study English, before going to Japan.

"I am grateful for my twenty years in America"

Just as Fr. Giorgio Paleari speaks with passion about his American experience, so too Fr. Giulio Mariani, currently regional superior of PIME in the Philippines, has a special place in his heart for the United States.[1] Says Fr. Giulio:

> When talking about PIME in America, some people think only about money and the aid sent to the missions, or about the number of American PIME members. But another important aspect also needs to be considered. About 140 missionaries have come to America from Italy, India and Brazil for different periods of work or study. We have to ask what advantages this brought to them. I spent 20 years in the States (1954–1974) and I am deeply grateful to PIME for having sent me there to study and to work. I learned English very well: today I think and speak more easily in English than in Italian; when I make notes for sermons or other talks, I automatically write them in English. In today's world, this is not a small thing for a missionary.
>
> It also helped me a lot to meet the members of Protestant denominations and to learn about ecumenism, not from books,

---

[1]Interviewed in Milan on April 22, 1997.

but in everyday life. I became good friends with a Methodist pastor who often invited me to preach and to comment on the Gospel at his parish. I was happy because this encounter with Protestant believers opened my mind and heart. At that time I was rector of the seminary in Newark (Ohio), and we used to take our seminarians to volunteer at the Methodist outreach program for poor children.

So for me it was a precious experience of opening up to others. Today an Italian who stays in Italy appears to me to be quite provincial, with a closed mentality. Now I am in love with the Philippines, because when I was younger I was in love with America. Isn't this the missionary spirit?

I am an American citizen and I have my criticisms about America also, especially in regard to the political sphere, but I like the American spirit and have learned much: it's a concrete, practical, and organized spirit, which is also universal, open, free and respectful of the liberty of others. America has taught me much and I sometimes think that all the Italian missionaries, at least those who are going to English speaking countries, should spend at least a year in the States to learn the language and this spirit of openness to the world.

In the summer of 1997, PIME in America gave hospitality to about a dozen missionaries of the institute and to native priests from the missions. Each year the missionaries destined for Asian countries where English is spoken come to the States for language study; they stay anywhere from six months to one or two years, often serving in a diocesan parish during their time here. Other missionaries come to America for sabbatical studies, to improve their English, or to preach mission appeals. Bishops and native priests of the missions founded by PIME are also frequent guests in our houses.

"The richness of America comes from the American spirit"

Father Nicholas Maestrini responds to my question: "What is the American spirit, and what can it teach us missionaries?"

> The American spirit has so many positive aspects. Many see America only in an external way, and think that the power of America is in its economic affluence. Instead, I think that the power resides in the "American spirit". The material affluence itself comes from the American spirit, which includes working hard to make use of the resources and gifts that God has given (many other countries have more raw materials than the United States and are considerably poorer). The American people are practical, concrete, organized, and hardworking. Sixteen and seventeen year olds work to pay for their studies, even if their families are wealthy. They do any kind of work, serving in restaurants, washing dishes, cutting lawns, delivering newspapers. etc.
>
> Another interesting aspect of the American spirit is collaboration for the common good. The Americans are much less individualistic than we Italians, because they are

taught from early on the importance of collaboration, working together. In America, the "team" is important, one for all and all for one, following a recognized leader; each knows his role. At the same time, there is a sense of integration, each one remaining who he is, with respect for the freedom and choices of others. Of course, divisions and racism still exist, but all consider themselves Americans and they find strength in American law.

Finally America teaches you to think big, to plan big; there is an optimistic attitude, open to the future and not tied to the past. There are missionaries who remain provincial, who think small, who have a limited vision. I want to add that not only the society but also the American church has much to teach us. This is being recognized by the young Italian missionaries, who come to study English and often reside in American parishes. They see, especially, the collaboration and dedication of the laity in the parish ministry, as well as the entire organization and efficiency of the pastoral services.

Instilling the missionary ideal in the North American church

The presence of PIME in North America is significant for the church here as well. We must be convinced of our charism and attempt to instill missionary ideals among North American Catholics. Besides missionary promotion, we do this with the witness of our lives.

Fr. Edward Miley says:

PIME members have a good missionary

spirit; I believe that our presence in North America enriches this church. The good American priest has three main priorities: administration and fund-raising; maintenance and repair of the church buildings and property; and service of the people with love and dedication. Everything is well-organized, according to times and schedules, which are followed consistently, except in cases of emergency. I have always admired the spirit of the PIME missionaries, who place themselves at the service of the people without regard to schedules and without any kind of reserve; for me, this is the missionary spirit.

In the beginning PIME came here to seek financial assistance for the missions and the institute, which were then in a state of real poverty, and appeals are still made for this purpose. But today our priority is vocations and the missionary formation of the American young people who come to us. This is the gift that we give to the American church.

I think the fact that we have lost many American priests is due to this: PIME was not able instill in the American young people, during their formation, this passion and zeal for the missions. They were not prepared for the difficulties of the missionary vocation; additionally, living practically alone in the missions (in foreign surroundings and with only Italian confreres with whom it is not easy to communicate on a deep, spiritual level), proved most difficult for them. Many of our American priests soon returned from the missions and are priests in the their own dioceses. In general you could say that we have been formed as good priests, but not necessarily as missionaries. This is the challenge that PIME must continue to face in America.

Fr. Ronald Boccali, in America since 1961, adds:

The spirituality of the American priest is different than ours. They are more active, more concrete. They don't spend much time in church, because for them work is prayer. I know many excellent American priests, who live an intense spiritual life and are more progressive and open than our Italians. For example, they know how to involve the laity, while we are more clerical. They also have a different style in regard to prayer and the life of faith. I don't judge one way better or worse than the other, but it's important to note the difference.

Fr. Amedeo Barbieri taught Sacred Scripture in America for twenty years. He says:

The Americans are more practical and concrete than we are, less accustomed to philosophy and metaphysics. To us they might seem superficial in their faith and piety, but I believe it is simply a matter of a different style of Christian life than ours. For example, a piety which is detached from life, common in Italy, doesn't exist in America. Piety either becomes life, or else it has no value.

I think that American Christians

reached the modern world before we did, that we have remained a bit behind, so that today we find ourselves a bit mystified by American spirituality, which is perhaps more current than ours, more in tune with the demands of our world. Naturally they also have their limitations as we do. But we should still understand them and, in the formation of missionaries in America, do away with that which is not admissible, but accept that which is positive, even if different from our style. I know that I'm speaking in very general terms, but I only want to point out how complex the issue is and how difficult it is to make judgments.

"The priesthood is not a 'job', but a mission"

Fr. Nicholas Maestrini depicts the service that the charism of PIME can give to America in this way:

I have known different American missionaries in China and Hong Kong and I have always admired them. I recall some Maryknoll missionaries, like Bishop James Walsh, Fr. Francis X. Ford, and Fr. John Considine, whom I considered to be true saints. Just think about this: Fr. Donald Hessler and Fr. Bernard Mayer were in Japanese concentration camps during World War II; as priests, thanks to an agreement between Japan and the Red Cross, they had the chance to be released and return to America. Instead, they chose to remain, at the risk of their own lives, to serve the English, American, Irish, Australian and Canadian Catholics detained

171

there. This is true heroism.

In regard to spirituality, we need to make clear that America is an eminently concrete, practical, and pragmatic country, so the spiritual life as we understand it takes second place.

Cardinal Joseph Bernardin, archbishop of Chicago from 1982 to 1996 when he died of cancer, sincerely admits in his best-selling book, *The Gift of Peace,* that he discovered the interior life of prayer only after he was already a bishop. He writes: "I was not used to reserving an adequate period of time for personal prayer. It's not that I lacked the desire to pray nor that I suddenly decided that the prayer was not important. But, being very busy, I had fallen into the trap of thinking that my good works were more important than prayer."

This is the reason that Cardinal Mooney told us that we must educate the American young people in the missionary spirit that he had seen in the Italian missionaries of PIME in India and Burma: not to make them into Italians, but to instill in them our spirit of prayer and devotion to the people.

Fr. Jim Coleman adds another element to the discussion He says:

PIME gives much to the American church. For instance, there is the example of orthodoxy, fidelity, respect and love for the pope and for the tradition of the church. This is an important witness here in America, where a certain anti-Rome spirit can be detected. There is also an exceptional example of devotion to the gospel. I believe that the vast majority of the PIME missionaries teach with their lives that the priesthood is not a "job," but a way of life. For some American priests the priesthood is a "job," with fixed schedules, functions to complete, buildings to manage. The missionaries of PIME are different and the friends of PIME see this, they experience it.

What are the feelings of the American PIME members?

In the past, the situation was not easy for American members of PIME (nor for Brazilian and Indian members), given the continual uncertainty in regard to the internationalization of the institute. The Italian members were slow to accept what it means to be international, namely, the difficulties encountered and the good will needed on everyone's part to overcome them.

In recent years this situation has improved, beginning with the General Assembly of 1989 in Tagaytay (Philippines) which established with clarity, once and for all, that PIME is international, without limits of any kind. Superior general, Fr. Franco Cagnasso, (elected in 1989 and reelected for a second six-year term in 1995) is very committed to this process of internationality. Nearly 150 years after its foundation (1850), PIME has chosen the most logical path for a missionary institute in modern times: internationality, intercultural living, an expanded world view. Says Fr. Kenneth Mazur:

Everyone in PIME should accept the fact that we are international,and that we have missionaries from many countries, races, and languages. Last month, I went to Italy, where I hadn't visited for six years, and I saw that Italy too is becoming a multi-racial and multi-cultural society. There are Africans, Chinese, Arabs, Filipinos, Indians, and Latin Americans everywhere. America is about a half century ahead of you in this regard and can teach something about the acceptance of different peoples, each of whom remain who they are. This is how I see the PIME of the future: living and working together while remaining different. However, I would say that the missionaries of a given country should be together as much as possible. I speak Italian well, but living in an Italian mission is not relaxing and not only because of the language. There are three of us Americans in Japan, but we're spread out in different areas. Why?

I am convinced that some of our American missionaries left the institute and went to their dioceses precisely for this reason; the same for some of our seminarians who left and joined the diocesan seminary. Still, I am optimistic for the future, because I see that the consciousness of internationality is growing a little bit in everyone.

The same idea is expressed by Fr. Tim Sattler:

I was in Manaus (the Brazilian Amazon) for six years. There was an American priest in Maués (Fr. John Majka) and another in Parintins (Fr. Jim Coleman); and when Fr. Dennis Koltz came to the Amazon, he was sent to Macapà. I didn't understand why we were not placed together, or at least nearby. As for the American region of PIME, in recent years, things have become better; the concept of authority has changed. Today we discuss things very well, and we all feel responsible. There is no fear about putting all the problems on the table for discussion.

I asked Fr. Sattler if he thinks that the Italian PIME members in the United States have not become "americanized" enough. He responded:

Some diocesan priests say that. Our fathers go to preach, but at times the people don't understand them. There was a missionary (now deceased) who had worked in Hong Kong, and who claimed to know more English words than any American. This might have been true, because he knew the language and vocabulary very well; but when he spoke, the people didn't understand him, not only because of his accent, but because his content was not relevant to their experience.

Guy Snyder is a student of theology at PIME's international seminary in Monza. He was ordaned a deacon in 1997. He says:

I've only been in PIME for a few years, but the experience that we Americans have in the Monza seminary is very beautiful. To live and study with Italians, Brazilians, Indians and those of other nationalities has helped me understand that to be a mis-

175

sionary means to live and work with those different from myself: not only Italian and not only white, but of any race, language, culture, or color. This also involves suffering, and in the beginning it's hard work, but then it becomes enriching. I believe that Monza is a model for PIME which is becoming international.

"I believe in the future of PIME in North America"

Fr. Steve Baumbusch, who was U.S. regional superior of PIME (1989–1995) and is now the rector of the College Community in Detroit, manifests a certain amount of suffering in speaking about this theme, a sign that in his opinion the process of becoming an international institute has not yet been completed.

In a presentation given to PIME members involved in formation, he wrote:

> For many Americans PIME was not (and is not) "home"; that is, the place where one has a sense of belonging, of personal worth, of giving and receiving from each other, of sharing the hard and beautiful things in life, a place where diversity is valued and everyone is welcomed because everyone belongs... At worst we have felt like strangers in the our own community; at best we have been well treated guests, but not members of the family.[2]

Fr. Steve continues to reflect about the identity of

---

[2] See his presentation, "Internationality," given at the PIME formation meeting in Ducenta (Dec.17, 1996–Jan. 4, 1997), in *InforPime*; July, 1997, pp.22–35

the American members of PIME. For example, he told me in an interview: "The mission in Mexico has given to us Americans in PIME, a focus, an image of our identity and missionary calling." Then he puts forth the fundamental question, to which this chapter is dedicated: "As Americans, what do we have to offer to PIME?" Despite the difficulties, Fr. Steve does not at all decline to work to establish the institute in America and to help it become "ever more international, in structures and in mentality."

He says:

> I believe that PIME has a future in North America and this future goes well beyond the economic aspect, which is also important. Our presence here in North America is a missionary presence, like that of Maryknoll or other missionary institutes. We have a charism that North America needs, and we will never be numerous enough to exhaust the possibilities of the Catholic church in our country. I also believe that there are vocations for PIME here. We've spread the word, and planted many seeds of vocations, but we have been unable to gather the fruits. In recent years we have not had anyone dedicated to vocation work full-time. Those who were involved in it also had other jobs. Now, with Fr. Claudio Corti, we have at least one who can give his full attention to this important field of work. That hasn't been the case for quite some time.
>
> I am convinced, and I speak not theoretically but from experience, that PIME is attractive to American young people. We

have a long history, many great missionaries, martyrs, and saints who have founded dioceses and mission districts; there's an adventurous spirit in PIME, (like that of Fr. Clement Vismara[3]), a spirit of freedom, a spirit of disinterested service, that American youth like. We've done and are doing a good job of spreading the word about PIME through the magazine, videos and many other promotional initiatives. We wait in faith, expecting that, with the help of God, the fruits will come in many good American vocations.

---

[3]Fr. Clement Vismara (1897–1988), a hero of the First World War, was ordained in 1923, and spent 65 years in Burma. He died at the age of 91. He is invoked as "the protector of children" because he took in 250 orphans and abandoned handicapped children. He and his children were helped very much by the Foster Parents Mission Club operated by PIME in Detroit. On October 18, 1996 the archbishop of Milan, Cardinal Carlo Maria Martini, began his cause of canonization (of which the postulator is Fr. Piero Gheddo). Fr. Nicholas Maestrini is preparing his biography in English.

APPENDIX I

FROM REGIONAL PHENOMENON TO INTERNATIONAL INSTITUTE

THE WORLD OF PIME

Canada & USA •Detroit
ENGLAND
ITALY
ASIA
14
India
6 11 •13
8 9
7 10 12
Africa
South America
1
1 Mexico
2 Brazil
2 Brazil
3
4 5
3 Guinea-Bissau
4 Cameroon
5 Ivory Coast
6 Bangladesh
7 India
8 Myanmar
9 Thailand
10 Cambodia
11 Hong Kong/China
12 Philippines
13 Taiwan
14 Japan
15 Papua New Guinea
15

IN ITALY DURING THE LAST CENTURY, AS THE COUNTRY WAS IN the process of becoming one nation, a great missionary movement began in various places. Young seminarians were dreaming of far-off peoples; priests entertained notions of founding missionary societies; and even the pope, Pius IX, put forth the idea that the Italian church might create an institution for the evangelization of the world.

Just before the mid point of the century, the providential hand of God set to work to bring together varied regional energies toward a single goal in the person of Father Angelo Ramazzotti from Milan. The desire the pope expressed for a missionary institute was the motivation Ramazzotti needed to realize something he aspired to with all his heart since his youth, that is, a missionary enterprise that young seminarians could join.

It was just then that Ramazzotti was named bishop of Pavia near Milan. With an innate genius, he got other bishops from the region involved in founding the "Institute for Foreign Missions" (December 1, 1850). These bishops knew it was the duty of each local church to extend the universal church by contributing apostolic personnel to such an institute.

From the very outset, the institute was characterized by a concern for evangelization especially of non-Christian people groups. The initial heroic response was to choose one of the most difficult missions in the Pacific islands, north of Australia. But they had to abandon it after a few years. Immediately they went to other areas of apostolate in Asia, the continent which most characterizes the option and style of the PIME Missionaries.

In 1926, Pope Pius XI combined the institute with another similar one which started in Rome in 1870: the Pontifical Seminary of Saints Peter and Paul for the Foreign Missions. The new entity became known as the Pontifical Institute for Foreign Missions.

In recent years PIME has opened other missionary fields in Asia, as well as returning to its original mission in Papua New Guinea. At the same time, the Institute began works in Africa and Latin America.

PIME has founded many dioceses in a spirit of

missionary service to local churches. Today PIME is receiving vocations from India, the United States, and Brazil, and is becoming increasingly international in membership.

UNITED STATES REGION MISSION STATEMENT

We, the PIME Missionaries of the United States Region, are an expression of the missionary nature of the Church in the United States and of the international character of PIME We are a family of apostles committed to the ongoing discovery, witness and proclamation of the Kingdom of God through evangelization, particularly of non-Christians in other parts of the world.

We live in community, offering one another mutual support. We work as a team, while respecting and encouraging individual initiative and creativity. We embrace a simple and hospitable lifestyle.

We work to establish the Kingdom through missionary evangelization, first and foremost, by preparing, sending and supporting missionaries, including clerical and lay associates. We also work to raise missionary concern and awareness within the U.S. Church, in collaboration and dialogue with other missionary groups and all people of good will. We maintain an option for the poor and concern for justice and peace issues.

We strive to be full of optimism and hope giving glory to God and obtaining personal sanctification through total commitment to our missionary calling.

APPENDIX II

THE MISSION OFFICE AND PROMOTION CENTER

STIMULATING RESPONSE TO GOD'S CALL TO MISSION IS WHAT the Mission Office and Promotion Center is all about in Detroit. This involves disseminating information and educating about the financial and spiritual needs where PIME missionaries labor. More importantly, it is about prayer and keeping the extended PIME family together. Following are some of the services and fund-raising events:

• **Leprosy Relief Society (LRS)** —

Founded in 1960, the LRS has aided people with Hansen's disease in Myanmar (formerly called Burma), Thailand, Bangladesh, India, Cameroon (in West Africa), and Brazil. PIME hospitals and treatment centers successfully cure persons with the disease and work to educate people about the cure. Once cured, the person, whom society often stigmatizes, gets help from PIME through job rehabilitation and housing.

• **PIME Chapels** —

PIME benefactors can contribute toward the building of chapels for poor communities. Chapels are often built in memory of loved ones.

• **Native Seminarians Program** —

Contributors to this program help poor dioceses educate their priests. Often it is even possible to adopt a specific young man.

- **Catechist Program —**

A way to support the important teaching function of local catechists. Such catechists are vital links between the missionary and the people being evangelized. They do everything from teach catechism to preside at paraliturgical functions when no priest is available.

- **Foster Parent Mission Club (FPMC) —**

Sponsorship of a child's education and formation is offered for ten dollars a month. PIME missionaries provide totally for the welfare of thousands of children in Asia, Africa and Latin America. PIME supporters make it possible. Regular gifts of only ten dollars go a long way in poor countries, and, because FPMC works directly with missionaries and hires no staff overseas, most of the money is used for the children.

- **Burses to educate a seminarian —**

Help finance the cost of educating a PIME seminarian by contributing to a special fund or burse.

- **Prayer Partnership —**

Behind everything that PIME does is prayer — the prayer of its members on the field and the committed praying relationship of the extended PIME family, those who support the missionaries. The PIME Prayer Partnership is a mutual compact made between missionaries and individual supporters. Both parties agree to fifteen minutes of prayer daily for the person they are in partnership with.

- **PIME Golf Day**

The annual PIME Golf Day was begun in 1957 by Frank D. Stella and Thomas V. Angott, prominent Detroit businessmen, to aid PIME in raising funds for educating its seminarians. It has continued growing over the years, due to the efforts of a generous committee of businessmen.

183

• Knights of Charity Award Dinner

The Knights of Charity Award Dinner has become an annual ecumenical event honoring persons who distinguish themselves by their charity. Started in 1954 by a committee of friends of PIME, encouraged and motivated by Father Nicholas Maestrini, the event has not only raised a great deal of support for PIME, but has contributed to interfaith understanding as well. One of the original organizers of the event, Judge Robert De Mascio, chaired the dinner committee for 1997. One of the three persons to be awarded was Mr. Frank D. Stella, who chaired the event for a decade along with Mr. Thomas V. Angott.

SUBSCRIBE TO PIME WORLD

When you subscribe to *PIME World* magazine, you become part of the extended family of PIME You will learn about the world of PIME — a world centered around the proclamation of the Gospel of Jesus Christ. *PIME World*, published ten times a year, contains photo stories and reports from PIME missionaries and others from around the world.To subscribe to *PIME World*, send five dollars and your name and address to:

PIME World
c/o PIME Missionaries
17330 Quincy Street
Detroit, MI 48221-2765

As a subscriber to *PIME World* you automatically become a benefactor of the works of the PIME Missionaries. As such, you are included in the prayers and Masses offered for the PIME "extended family."

APPENDIX III

PIME IN
NORTH AMERICA

THE PIME CENTERS IN NORTH AMERICA ARE PRESENT TO PRO-
mote Christ's mission in the Catholic church and to re-
cruit and train for foreign missions. PIME's mission is to:
• Establish the Kingdom of God by evangelizing
• Engage in human development
• Promote justice and peace
• Educate
• Care for the sick
• Aid the poor and children
• Dialogue with other religions
• Be present as a Christian witness around the world
    Following are the PIME centers in the United
States, Canada and Mexico:

MICHIGAN

PIME Regional Headquarters
17330 Quincy Street
Detroit, Michigan 48221-2765
Phone: (313) 342-4066
Fax: (313) 342-6816
E-mail: pimeusa@aol.com
Web site:
http://www.rc.net/pime
Also located at the above address are:
• PIME Mission & Promotion Center
• PIME College Community and Vocation Office
• PIME World Publications

San Francesco Parish
22780 S. Nunnely Road
Mt. Clemens,
Michigan 48043
Phone: (810) 792-5346
Fax: (810) 792-5119

OHIO

PIME Mission Center
2734 Seminary Road, S.E.
Newark, Ohio 43055
Phone: (614) 928-4246
Fax: (614) 928-1512

FLORIDA

PIME Mission House
1550 Beach Road
Tequesta, Florida 33469
Phone: (516) 746-7767
Fax: (516) 747-9549
E-mail: nichom@aol.com

NEW JERSEY

PIME Mission House
34 Grandview Drive
Wayne, New Jersey 07470
Phone: (201) 694-1790
Fax: (201) 694-0444
E-mail: pimeusanj@aol.com

MEXICO

Misioneros del PIME
Casa Parroquial
Art. 123 1B
41603 San Luis Acatlán,
Guerrero
Mexico

TORONTO, CANADA

Blessed Agnes Tsao Kouying
Catholic Mission
183 Valleymede Drive
Richmond Hill, Ontario
L4B 3J5 Canada
Phone: (905) 881-5633
Fax: (905) 889-4824

BECOMING A PIME MISSIONARY PRIEST

Anyone interested in a career as a missionary priest may contact any of the above centers or write for information to:

PIME Vocation Director
17330 Quincy St.
Detroit, Michigan 48221-2765

Depending on the educational background of the person accepted by PIME for missionary formation and ordination to the priesthood, he will first attend the University of Detroit Mercy for undergraduate studies. Also part of the training is a mission-exposure trip to give the candidate a taste of life in a mission, and a year of spirituality, a time to concentrate on one's personal relationship with God and to learn about the PIME history and tradition. The final four years of study take place at an international school of theology in Monza, Italy. Here, men from several countries of the world come together to complete their formation before ordination while sharing their own experiences and world view with other students.

APPENDIX IV

PIME WORLD PRESS BOOKS AND PAMPHLETS

Crimson Seeds: Eighteen PIME Martyrs by Mariagrazia Zambon (translated by Steve Baumbusch, PIME, from the Italian original, *A Causa di Gesu*). The life and death stories of the men who were killed in the service of the Lord. 212 pages. 1997. $10.00

Gold in the Mountains: The Mountain Tribes of Thailand by Corrado Ciceri, PIME, and Dino Vanin, PIME. Facts, color photos and map, stories — all telling the story of how PIME missionaries relate to the colorful mountain tribes people of Thailand. 88 pages. 1996. $8.00

Forever Love: God's Plan for Happiness by Nicholas Maestrini, PIME. Spirituality for today, the result of the long working experience of a priest and missionary. 294 pages. 1996. $12.00

Good News at 7:18 by Piero Gheddo, PIME. Mission experiences and Gospel meditation. (Based upon the Italian original, *Vangelo delle 7:18*.) 108 pages. 1996. $7.00

China: Lost Mission? by Nicholas Maestrini, PIME. A bittersweet account of mission in China from 1931 to 1951 told from the personal perspective of Father Maestrini (also available in Italian under the title, *Cina: Missione Fallita?*). 374 pages. 1992. $12.00

P.I.M.E. in the United States, the First Twenty-five Years, 1947–1972 by Nicholas Maestrini, PIME. 354 pages. 1994. Limited availability.

Vocation: A Reflection by Franco Cagnasso, Superior General of PIME. 17 pages. $3.50

A Missionary Way of the Cross by Steve Baumbusch, PIME. $1.50

BOOKS AND PAMPHLETS AVAILABLE

through PIME World Press

No Greater Love by Carlo Suigo, PIME. The story of Blessed John Mazzucconi. 62 pages. 1962. $2.00

Lawrence Bianchi of Hong Kong by Piero Gheddo, PIME. The life of the last Western bishop of Hong Kong. (Published by the Catholic Truth Society of Hong Kong.) 215 pages. 1992. $10.00

Apostolic Virtues by Paolo Manna, PIME. A collection of letters by a former Superior General whose spiritual insights and leadership were substantial. (Translated from the Italian, *Virtu Apostoliche* by Steve Baumbusch, PIME.) 245 pages. 1996. Limited availability.

Apostle of the Karens, Venerable Fr. Paolo Manna by Father Edward P. Evans. 74 pages. 1996

PIME AUDIOVISUALS

VHS VIDEOS

Papua New Guinea, the Farthest Mission. A look at current PIME mission in Oceania. Length: 38 minutes. $15.00

Manaus, in the Heart of the Amazon. The struggle of the poor on the Brazilian frontier. Length: 32 minutes. $15.00

Angels of Misery, Street Children in Brazil. Length: 27 minutes. $15.00

Hong Kong — What Does the Future Hold? The Church in Hong Kong now and after 1997. Length: 27 minutes. $15.00

Distant Neighbors, PIME'S Mission among the Mixtec. PIME's Mexico mission. Length: 34 minutes. $15.00

Faith in the Amazon. The candle of Nazareth Procession in Belen, Brazil. Length: 19:40 minutes. $15.00

The Little Ones. About Asia's children in the 1950s. Length: 23:16 minutes. $12.00

The Touch of His Hand. About Father Caesar Colombo and the beginning of leprosy relief in Burma. Length: 42:34 minutes. $12.00

The Happy City. Sequel to the *The Touch of His Hand.* Length: 36:04 minutes. $12.00

Latitude Zero. Early PIME mission in the Amazon. Length: 22 minutes. $12.00

Make a Difference! You Can Do Great Things with Your Life. PIME vocational video. 12:14 min. Free

OTHER BOOKS

U.S. publications by or about PIME missionaries not currently available

Forward with Christ, Thoughts and Reflections on Vocations to the Foreign Missions by Father Paul Manna, PIME. (Adapted by Nicholas Maestrini, PIME.) Newman Press, Maryland. 163 pages. 1954

In *God's Hands, the Life of Blessed Alberic Crescitelli, Priest and Martyr* by Elio Gasperetti. 87 pages. 1955

The Touch of His Hands, A Modern Day Damien in

Burma. Biography of Father Cesar Colombo, PIME by Jean Maddern Pitrone. Alba House, New York. 161 pages. 1970

The Cross and the Bo-tree, Catholics and Buddhists in Vietnam by Piero Gheddo, PIME. Sheed and Ward, New York. 369 pages. 1970

Why is the Third World Poor? by Piero Gheddo, PIME. Orbis Books, Maryknoll. 143 pages. 1973

Mazzucconi of Woodlark, the Life of Blessed John Mazzucconi, Priest and Martyr by Nicholas Maestrini, PIME. 216 pages.1983

P'eng P'ai and the Hai-Lu-Feng Soviet by Fernando Galbiati, PIME. Stanford University Press, California. 324 pages. 1985

Available from the author

Water from the Old Fountain by Casto Marrapese, PIME. A collection of sermons. 198 pages